H E P
REMEMBERED

Memories of Terry Hoeppner from Those Who Knew Him Best

Terry Hutchens

Foreword by Ben Roethlisberger

Blue River Press
Indianapolis, Indiana

Hep Remembered © 2007 Terry Hutchens

Cover designed by Phil Velikan
Cover photos and interior photos of Indiana University players and coaches by Paul Riley of Indiana University
Photos of Miami of Ohio players and coaches appear courtesy of the Miami of Ohio athletic department
Photo in the "Just for Kicks" chapter provided by Jane Hoeppner

Printed in the United States of America
10 9 8 7 6 5 4 3 2 1

Published by Blue River Press

Distributed by Cardinal Publishers Group
2222 Hillside Avenue, Suite 100
Indianapolis, Indiana 46218
www.cardinalpub.com

This book is lovingly dedicated to the memory of my father, Al Hutchens, who reminded me a lot of Hep. He was a wonderful husband, father and grandfather, who cherished the time he spent with his family. Like Hep, he was hard-working and passionate and was taken from this earth long before his time.

Preface & Acknowledgments

In late October of 2006, about three weeks after Terry Hoeppner returned to the Indiana football team following his second brain surgery, I asked Hep if he thought he might be interested in writing a book together about his fight with brain cancer. The working title was something along the line of "Don't Ever Quit: My Victory over Brain Cancer." We probably talked about it a total of two or three times, but each time he had that gleam in his eye that made me think this was a project he'd like to pursue. Unfortunately, we never got very far. After Hep died on June 19, 2007, I kept feeling I was being called to write a book as a tribute to a great man who touched so many people. It became a whirlwind project, but as I step back and look at the body of work, I tell myself that Hep's story was one that needed to be told.

I want to thank many people for helping me make this a reality. Tom Doherty with Cardinal Publishers Group jumped on board and got it on the shelves quickly. I also want to thank him for agreeing to give a percentage of the profits from the book to an Indiana scholarship fund in the name of Terry Hoeppner. Mark Bast agreed to edit the project and was both extremely professional and easy to work with. Holly Kondras handled the layout, pagination and photos. My supervisors at the *Indianapolis Star* gave me the OK to write this during the college football season, which I appre-

Opposite page: Located on State Road 37 on the outskirts of Bloomington, this billboard welcomed Coach Hep to town.

v

ciate very much. I'd like to thank Indiana University media relations directors J.D. Campbell and Jeff Keag for their support during this project. Associate A.D. Tim Fitzpatrick was supportive from the administrative end. In addition, IU photographer Paul Riley, who took the majority of the photos that appear in this book, was also passionate in his cooperation. He was one of a long list of people who were deeply touched by Terry Hoeppner and eager to give something back. I'd also like to thank Dawn Clark in the Miami of Ohio football office for sending me pictures of Hep at Miami.

Bill Lynch, his coaching staff and the Indiana players were open and cooperative. When I interviewed Lynch the first time, I was ten minutes late and he told me he was going to make me run gassers at the end of practice. I told him I was wearing sandals and not real excited about running, and he said, "OK, I guess we'll have to settle for sit ups and push ups." Thankfully, he never followed through. All of the assistant coaches were helpful. I want to single out Bobby Johnson and Joe Palcic, who were helpful in getting me together with former Miami players. Brian George and Billy Lynch offered some humorous stories about Hep. IU Varsity Club director Scott Dolson and assistant director Kelly Bomba were also invaluable in helping me track down a source or two to interview.

I could never even think about a project like this without the support of my wife, Susan, and my teenage boys, Bryan and Kevin. They had to endure my divided attention.

I want to thank all of the people who allowed me to interview them. Specifically, I want to thank Ben Roethlisberger for working with me inseason, which I'm certain was an inconvenience. I'd also like to thank his agent, Ryan Tollner, for helping me hook up with Ben.

Most of all, I want to thank the Hoeppner family and especially Terry's wife, Jane, for giving me her blessing when I first thought about this book. If Jane hadn't been behind it, I never would have tried it. She's very much the personification of the thought that behind every great man is an equally great woman. Hep was a warrior, and Jane was right there at his side every step of the way.

His children are living proof that the apple doesn't fall far from the tree. I want to thank Drew, Amy and Allison for their support in this endeavor as well. Finally, I want to thank Hep himself for the inspiration he provided. Not a day goes by that I don't hear one of Hep's sayings echoing in my ears. "Have a plan. Work the plan. Plan for the unexpected," could have been the theme for this book as I tried to pull things together at a very quick pace. Hep gave us all a reason to hope and believe that above everything else in life, we simply can never allow ourselves to quit.

— Terry Hutchens

Table of Contents

Opposite page: Coach Hep with grandson Quinn Balcam at Memorial Stadium.

Foreword

by Ben Roethlisberger

Everybody has a story about Coach Hep. You'll read a lot of great ones in this book. I have dozens of them. He was just one of those guys you wanted to be around because of his passion and enthusiasm. I know I did. He was the first coach that showed an interest in me, and Miami of Ohio was the first school that recruited me. When I decided to play at Miami, the fact that they were the first to offer me a scholarship was important. It showed that he had faith in me, he believed in me, and he trusted that I was going to be able to succeed. I'll never forget when Coach Hep came to our house. This was when (current New York Jets quarterback) Chad Pennington was either at Marshall or had just left. In any case, he had done unbelievable things there. And Coach Hep said to my family and me that he thought I could be the next Chad Pennington – only better. He was a heck of a salesman. If he believed in it, he'd talk you into it. He told me about the player he thought I could become, and I believed him.

Coach Hep taught me so many lessons in life, and I will forever be grateful for all that he did for me both as a football player and a man. I think what he taught me more than anything else was simply how to live life. He showed me how to smile in the face of adversity. People always get on me because I'll throw an interception and start laughing, or I'll

Ben Roethlisberger (left) stands on the sidelines with Terry Hoeppner at Indiana-Wisconsin game, Sept. 30, 2006, at Memorial Stadium. Hoeppner had his second brain surgery 17 days earlier.

shake my head and flash this big smile. They think I should be more serious or more remorseful. But what I tell them is, "You know what? I can't take it back." There's nothing I can do about it. I made a mistake. It's over. Time to move on. So many times, coach Hep smiled in the face of adversity. And he'd say, "You know what? This is what was dealt to me. What can I do to improve it? What can I do to make sure it doesn't happen again? If it was a mistake I made, what can I do to correct it?" That's what Hep taught me. He taught me to smile when things are going well, but also when they're not. He taught me to love life and to love people that love you. The longer I was out of school and the older I got, the more I grew to love and respect him.

After I left Miami of Ohio and went on to play for the Steelers, our relationship blossomed that much more. We would talk once a week, before my game and his, usually on Fridays. We'd quickly talk about the upcoming games, and then turn to everything non-football for who knows how long. We could talk about anything – and usually did. Whenever I've needed advice or had questions about anything, I've always been able to go to my own dad. But in a lot of those cases I'd go to Coach Hep, too, because I really saw him as a father figure and someone who would do anything for me. My dad had a great deal of respect for Coach Hoeppner as well. He would be the first to tell you that there could be no better second father to his son than Coach Hep.

When Coach Hoeppner started having the headaches that led to his first brain surgery, he had just come to see me play against the Browns in Cleveland. It was late December in 2005. He was on the field with me for both pre-game and post-game and looked great. I can't remember exactly when he called me, but it was a few days later, and he said he had been having headaches and that it turned out he had a brain tumor that was going to require surgery. I remember him saying, "But you know Ben, it's no big deal." And it's hard to explain, but what he was saying didn't really sink in. I don't know if it's because he played it so cool, but I completely believed it wasn't a big deal. See, this was Coach Hep. I always believed he was invincible. So I just figured it was something he had to do, that he would fight it, and he would beat it. Like he said, "It's not a big deal. I'll be playing golf in no time." So, in a lot of ways the brain cancer never sunk in for me. It didn't really hit me until it got so bad that he couldn't get out of the hospital.

I think one of the reasons Hep always seemed larger than life was the way he bounced back. A month after his first surgery, he was with me when we played in the Super Bowl. A few weeks after his second surgery, it was our bye week, and I was with him at Indiana when he returned to coach his team against Wisconsin. And in both of those cases, he looked absolutely terrific. If you didn't know differently, you would never have guessed what he had been through.

I feel so lucky that he and I got to share so much before he died. I look back and I'm so grateful that I got to win the Super Bowl so early, with him there. He was with me the day I was drafted into the NFL. I'm going to miss him not being at another Super Bowl if we get that chance again. Even more so, I'm going to miss him not being in the front row when I get married someday.

On game days in the NFL, I write the initials "KCR" on my wristband for Kenneth Carl Roethlisberger, my grandfather who died in 2005. And then I write "HEP." It's on my wristband with our plays, and every time I check a play I see those initials. And it makes me feel good to think about both of those men who meant so much to me. Before every game I play now, I kneel down at the 20-yard line and say a quick prayer. I tell my grandfather to watch over me, and I tell Coach Hep to sit back and enjoy the show.

Chapter 1
Hep

Terry Hoeppner was only the head football coach at Indiana University for 914 days. He never had a winning season, never took the Hoosiers to a bowl game, and never had a chance to realize the majority of the hopes and dreams he had for the university's football program.

But he made a difference.

In just over two seasons as the IU head coach, he was credited with changing the culture and the landscape of Indiana football. He got players and fans alike believing that you could have a successful football program in Bloomington after so many years of apathy and lethargy.

He captured the hearts of Indiana students, who for over a decade stayed away from Memorial Stadium in droves on Saturday afternoons. He began the tradition of calling the stadium "The Rock" by placing a large three-ton chunk of limestone from the original stadium at the north end zone. It became a symbol that IU players thought worth fighting for, and the coaches openly challenged players to "Defend the Rock."

He started the "Walk to the Rock," a game-day procession that starts a few blocks from Memorial Stadium and parades IU players through the tailgating areas, with fans and well-wishers lining both sides of the route. In addition, he established the tradition of IU coaches and players joining The Marching Hundred band to sing the school fight song after every home victory. Most of all, his energy, passion and enthusiasm for Indiana football was infectious. Terry Hoeppner put IU football back on the map.

"This football program was as low as it had ever been," said long-time IU football and basketball broadcaster Don Fischer. "Not because of (former coach) Gerry DiNardo, but because of what we had gone through for the last eleven years. We were coming off three seasons in which we had won a total of eight games, and nobody was showing up. We had announced crowds of 27,000 in the stands, and everybody knew there were no more than 15-17,000. And I'm talking game after game.

"I had never seen the Indiana program at the depths it was when Hep took over. And almost instantly he transformed Indiana fans' thinking. 'You know what?' they started saying. 'This guy might get it done.' What he brought initially was his enthusiasm and energy, and in his mind there was never any doubt that he could be successful at IU. There haven't been many people involved with IU football who can say that. Terry Hoeppner was clearly one of the few."

✯ ✯ ✯

Terry Hoeppner was named the Indiana University football coach on December 17, 2004. He had spent the previous nineteen seasons as a coach at Miami of Ohio, in Oxford, Ohio. The last six seasons, with Hoeppner as head coach, his teams went 48-25. In 2003, his Miami team was ranked tenth in the final Associated Press poll and rated as high as eleventh in the Bowl Championship Series. That team finished 13-1 and won the GMAC Bowl. In 2004, the season before he took the IU job, the RedHawks were 8-5 and played in the Independence Bowl.

Hoeppner had finally arrived the day he was introduced as the twenty-sixth head football coach in Indiana University history. A born and bred Hoosier who attended Woodlan High School in Woodburn, Ind., Hoeppner had never made any secret of the fact that the only job he could ever see himself leaving Miami for was Indiana. He received his undergraduate degree from Franklin College and his Masters of Education from Butler. He was Indiana through and through.

The IU job once seemed a long shot. In 2001, when IU fired Cam Cameron and eventually hired Gerry DiNardo, Hoeppner was more than a little interested in the IU job. But when his team lost a late-November game in Hawaii and then came back and dropped a makeup game from 9/11 to Kent State, any momentum he might have had was lost. Michael McNeely, IU's athletic director at the time, never called Miami for permission to speak to Hoeppner.

But when IU athletic director Rick Greenspan called to inquire of his interest in 2004, Hoeppner made it perfectly clear that his lifelong dream was to be the Indiana football coach. After a few conversations, Greenspan was pretty certain that he had found his man. It was a decision he would never regret. Terry Hoeppner was everything he wanted in an IU football coach, and much, much more.

On the day Hoeppner was introduced, a joking Greenspan brought out a crystal punch bowl holding a single rose and set it on the podium as Hoeppner began making his opening remarks. The message was that expectations were high and the athletic director was expecting Hoeppner to take the Hoosiers to just their second Rose Bowl appearance in history (the other was 1967). As Greenspan approached the podium to put the punch bowl away, Hoeppner motioned for his new boss to leave the bowl right there. Hoeppner was not afraid to dream.

When he was in junior high school Hep told his sister that one day he would be the head football coach at Indiana University. The day he accepted the job, he called his sister and told her that it had taken him forty years, but he had finally done it. He was the Hoosiers new head coach.

Standing at the podium, Hoeppner made all of the obligatory thank you's to the athletic administrators at both Indiana and Miami. Miami would always have a special place in his heart, he said, and relayed that all three of his children earned their degrees at MU. Then he got personal.

"There really is only one job that I would ever leave Miami for, and that is Indiana University," Hoeppner said. "IU is an opportunity that the voice inside my mind always said, 'Someday.' Well, that someday is now."

University of Minnesota athletic director Joel Maturi was the A.D. at Miami of Ohio when Coach Randy Walker left in 1999 to take the head coaching job at Northwestern. Maturi then promoted Hoeppner from his defensive coordinator role to head coach.

"I knew back then that Terry Hoeppner was the perfect fit to be the head coach at Miami, but I also knew that if the Indiana job ever became available, Hep would be the ideal man for that job, too," Maturi said. "When he called Indiana his dream job, I had no doubt that was true. It's not that he wasn't happy at Miami, because he was. But with Indiana, Hep was getting the chance to go home, and everyone knew that's where he wanted to be."

Greenspan talked to dozens of prospective candidates, and about ten received interviews. But in the end, he was certain he had the right guy. "The search process was national and open to those who applied," Greenspan said on the day Hoeppner was hired. "We were aggressive in our pursuit. However, in the end, the choice was easy. I thought it was time to add a Hoosier to Indiana football."

Hoeppner's course was charted for what would be an all too brief two-and-a-half-year ride at Indiana. "Indiana football presents a great opportunity and a great challenge," Hoeppner said. "We are accustomed to winning at Miami, and I want to carry that winning tradition over to the Big Ten. I know we can do that. We will build on the foundation already in place." He looked over at the crystal bowl with the single red rose and nodded his head. "Our goal is simple – the Rose Bowl. We will shoot for perfection and settle for excellence."

✯ ✯ ✯

Over the next eight months, long before Hoeppner ever coached his first game at IU, he put on his salesman hat and went recruiting. First he brought five assistants with him from Miami, a core of guys that would allow him to keep his old system in place, yet tweak it to adapt to the Indiana personnel. He got Bill Lynch to leave his head coaching job at DePauw and join him as assistant head coach. Then he re-recruited all of the Indiana players on the roster when he was hired. He singled out the seniors in particular and assured them he wasn't looking to kick them to the curb and win with younger players. He wanted them to have a positive experience in their final year.

Next he went full steam and filled up a twenty-four man recruiting class in less than six weeks. Ten of the fourteen recruits who had given verbal commitments to play for DiNardo opted to stay and play for Hoeppner. A few weeks before the class signed national letters of intent to play for IU, Hoeppner made it clear that recruiting from behind the eight ball hadn't been easy, but he was happy with the results. "It's not easy to play catch-up, but I'm not making excuses either," Hoeppner said. "I don't want a mulligan. I don't want a do-over. I think we can assemble a solid class right from the start."

Finally, he recruited the state of Indiana from top to bottom, side to side, and everywhere in between, as he sought to restore enthusiasm to the IU football program. The recruiting targets were IU alumni and fans, and that first year he made significant inroads with the IU Nation. By mid-March he had already begun. In an interview that month, he talked about his early experiences with IU fans.

"We've been recruiting them every day," Hoeppner said. "Whether it was speaking at a high school awards banquet on Monday night, or the High School Coaches Association Clinic on Friday night or the Bedford United Way on Saturday night, that's what happened this week. If you look at my calendar, it's filled up. I don't think I've refused a single speaking engagement. There's a lot of excitement around the program right now. We need to use that momentum and build on it. My plan is to do whatever I can to expose myself and the program to the community."

Over the course of that first year leading into the 2005 season, Hoeppner spoke to eighty-three different groups. He had pizza with students in their dormitories and invited representatives from IU's various fraternities and sororities to talk with him about improving student involvement. He spoke to service groups, retirement homes, anyone who wanted him. He never said "No." IU put together a "Coach Hep Wants You" advertising campaign, featuring the coach on billboards, radio and television. By the end of that first season the results were impressive. Indiana had enjoyed a thirty-nine percent increase in per-game attendance, a forty-six percent increase in overall season ticket sales, and a one hundred ten percent increase in student season ticket sales.

"I've said from day one that I like to be around people who have passion, and Terry exudes passion," IU athletic director Rick Greenspan said at the time. "I think it's contagious within an athletic department. People feed off it and he understands that. I don't think it's a sense of false personality. That's who he is."

But Hep was just getting started. He was happy with the early numbers but made it clear he thought IU had only scratched the surface of its potential. "I think it's a credit to our marketing people and the university for the commitment they have made to our football program," Hep told the *Indianapolis Star* in August of 2005. "But it's only a start. My goal is to more than double the season tickets we have sold. Some people think I've set my goals too high, but I don't think that's possible."

His fellow coaches knew what Hoeppner was capable of both on and off the field. To a man, they believed there was nothing he couldn't do. "If he wasn't a football coach, he could have made a ton of money doing a lot of other things," said IU assistant coach Billy Lynch. "I'm young, but I've never seen anyone get people to believe a vision and ideas like

Hep. Like my dad always said, 'Faith is belief without evidence.'

"Obviously the coaches and players believed in him because we saw him on a daily basis. But to get the fans and the people of Indiana talking about him shows what a powerful salesman he was. He could convince people without evidence, and that's not an easy thing to do."

Looking back on Hoeppner's time at Indiana, Rick Greenspan said months later that his football coach was a man who believed he could succeed in any situation. It didn't matter if it was coaching his team, recruiting players, or getting people excited about IU football.

"He had a real disappointment in his heart when he couldn't accomplish something," Greenspan said. "He thought, 'This state is not that big, and I'll convert people one at a time if I have to,' and if he had enough time, I'm convinced he probably would have done just that."

As a football coach, Hoeppner led the Hoosiers to a 4-7 record his first season in 2005, which included a 4-1 start. His second season, in 2006, the Hoosiers went 5-7. With three games to play, they were 5-4 and needed one victory to qualify for their first bowl game since 1993. But losses to Minnesota, Michigan and Purdue to end the season left the Indiana program on the outside looking in.

The 2006 season had some impressive wins, including a 31-28 victory over No. 13 Iowa and a 46-21 pounding of Michigan State. It also featured some gut-wrenching losses, including a 35-28 decision to NCAA Division I-AA Southern Illinois, a game Hoeppner missed because of surgery. IU also lost a nonconference home game to Connecticut, 14-7, the next week. Had the Hoosiers won either of those games, they would have played in a postseason bowl game.

A few days after IU's season came to an end with a 28-19 loss to Purdue, Hoeppner talked about the season. His biggest disappointment was for his seniors. "Seeing the seniors in the locker room would have moved anyone," Hoeppner said. "They put so much into it, and it was so important to

7

IU radio announcer Don Fischer (left) and Coach Hep at Hoeppner's weekly radio show.

them. All the rest of us will just wait until next year, but they can't do that. In some ways this has been a very satisfying year. The support, the opportunities afforded me, the players, the IU and Bloomington community, the state of Indiana. And of course the overwhelming support and enthusiasm of our fans.

"Did we accomplish everything that we could have? No. But we affected a lot of people. We've laid a foundation, and the spirit is great, not only with the team, but within the Hoosier Nation. I will return next year and for as long as they'll keep me around here, within reason. I'm not going to try to break Joe Paterno's longevity record."

That was November 21, 2006. Seven months later, Hoeppner died of complications from brain cancer and the IU Nation was left to mourn.

☆ ☆ ☆

Indiana University football was turned on its ear in late December of 2005 when it was revealed that Terry Hoeppner had undergone brain surgery at Bloomington Hospital.

Hoeppner first experienced headaches while attending the Pittsburgh-Cleveland NFL game in Cleveland on December 24 and watching his former pupil, Ben Roethlisberger, face the Browns. The day after Christmas, Hoeppner saw a doctor who confirmed that a scan had shown that the IU coach had a tumor on his brain. The next day, December 27, doctors removed the tumor and told Hoeppner they believed it hadn't spread. It was serious, but they never put a percentage on his chances for survival.

Instead of radiation treatment, Hoeppner was told he was a candidate for the less-invasive proton therapy, in which a proton beam is directed at the specific cancer area. Only three centers in the country perform that therapy – Loma Linda, California, Boston and Bloomington, Indiana.

"They were able to bombard the area with this proton by controlling the depth of the treatment," Hoeppner said in an interview with the *Indianapolis Star* a few months after the surgery. "Radiation is just like an X-ray. It goes right through you, so they have to use a lesser dose. But with this stuff, when they isolate the spot, they can turn up the juice and really go after it."

The treatments began the Monday after the Super Bowl and ended midway through spring practice. Shortly thereafter, doctors delivered the positive news that everything looked good. It was obvious at the time that Hoeppner hadn't lost his sense of humor, either. When the doctors gave him the good news, one told him he was perfect. Another said he was great, and a third said he was much better.

"So I'm somewhere between much better and perfect," Hoeppner told the *Star*. "When the doctor said perfect, I said, 'Wow, that's a lot better than I was before the surgery.'"

In May of 2006, Hoeppner continued to rest but was still maintaining as much of a normal life as possible. He was playing golf somewhat regularly and was seen on his jet ski on Lake Monroe. He wasn't pounding the pavement with speaking engagements, though, like he had done the year before.

In 2006 Hoeppner came to the realization that he was probably doing too much and needed to take a step back. "I was negotiating with my time," Hoeppner said in May of 2006. "I would say, 'OK, I'll do this, but I've got to do that.' I was always prioritizing everything but finding a way to still do just about all of it. That had been going on for a long, long time. I told myself last fall I wasn't going to do eighty-three events this summer – I was going to do eighty-four."

As the 2006 season approached, his second as the IU coach, Hoeppner was optimistic about his health and his team's chances. Summer practice went well, and before long the Hoosiers were opening the season with Western Michigan. Indiana won its first two games – against Western Michigan and Ball State – but football once again took a backseat for Hoeppner a few days after that victory over the Cardinals. On September 12, 2006, Hoeppner told his players that he must have a second brain surgery. He was hopeful that what they had seen on a scan was just scar tissue, but he didn't want to take any chances. The next day, on September 13, he had surgery once again at Bloomington Hospital.

Hoeppner would officially miss the next two games, but amazingly, he was able to sneak into one of the administrative boxes above the press box and watch both of them. The first one – against Southern Illinois – was three days after his surgery.

"There's no way I could have stayed away (from that first game)," Hoeppner said a few weeks later. "The surgeon said I could go if I didn't get too excited. In week two, I felt since I'd gone in week one, I didn't want the team to feel like I wasn't there. It was a different perspective to the game. I hadn't been in the press box for a game in twenty years. It gave me a 'big picture' sense of things, but I'd just as soon not have to do it again."

More amazingly, he was back on the sideline the following week when the Hoosiers opened Big Ten play on September 30 against Wisconsin. He actually rejoined the team on Sunday, September 24, eleven days after brain surgery.

"I think that's when all of the guys on our team realized that Hep was larger than life," said senior safety Will Meyers. "When he came back just a few weeks after his second brain surgery, it made all of us say to ourselves that if he could do that, then we could go the extra mile for him. I think that was a defining moment for our football team."

A few days after his second surgery, he appeared before the Indiana Board of Trustees during a presentation about athletic department facility improvements. Among those improvements was a plan to renovate and enclose the north end zone of Memorial Stadium. The plan also called for new offices, team rooms and a weight-lifting area. When Hoeppner walked into the meeting that day, there wasn't a dry eye in the place.

In his weekly press conference during the week before the Wisconsin game, Hoeppner talked about his second surgery and revealed that it was indeed only scar tissue. "They told me after the first surgery that there might be an element of scar tissue," Hoeppner said. "It happened to be Jane's birthday (last week), and she got scar tissue for her birthday. Right now, I'm good to go. The scan after the surgery was clear."

Hoeppner finished out the 2006 season without any health concerns, at least none that were made public. Next came a rigorous recruiting season that left Hoeppner mentally and physically exhausted. At national signing day on February 7, 2007, Hoeppner looked weak and actually had his assistant coaches do most of the talking about the new recruits. Little did anyone know, it was one of the final public appearances Hoeppner would make.

After the recruiting season, the IU coach took some time off to re-energize. In March, the university announced that Hoeppner would miss spring practice "to regain his strength and energy and to receive proper medical care."

Jane Hoeppner's statement read, "At this time, our family feels it is in Terry's best interest to step away from football for a time to concentrate on regaining his strength. We appreciate the thoughts and prayers of Indiana supporters throughout the nation."

If it wasn't bad enough that his health was requiring him to miss spring practice – one of his favorite times of the year – the fact that Hoeppner never made an appearance at IU during that time made everyone realize that his health situation must have taken a turn for the worse.

Over the next few months, there was little word regarding Hoeppner. On May 8, Hoeppner released a statement updating his health:

"We want to thank the many fans and friends who have sent their best wishes and thoughts to us over the past several weeks," Hoeppner said. "I continue to receive medical treatment and remain inspired to return to coaching when my health permits. I love Indiana University and Indiana football and will make decisions in the best interest of the program, as I have always attempted to do. I will ask for your continued respect for the privacy of me and my family as I address these matters going forward."

Five weeks later, on June 15, IU announced that Bill Lynch would coach the Indiana football team for the 2007 season, as Hoeppner continued his leave of absence. In the press release was a statement from Jane Hoeppner in which she acknowledged that her husband had been receiving chemotherapy and radiation treatments for the past several months. What Indiana didn't say was that Hoeppner was back in the hospital. He came home briefly, for less than twenty-four hours, and then was re-admitted on June 16.

Three days later, Terry Hoeppner died in Bloomington Hospital from brain cancer complications. He was 59.

Hoeppner died early on a Tuesday morning. His family opted to hold the memorial service on "Game Day" and held it Saturday in Bloomington's Assembly Hall. A crowd estimated at more than 5,000 attended the uplifting service that included speeches by Rick Greenspan, Anthony Thompson, Miami athletic director Brad Bates, IU wide receiver James Hardy, assistant coach Joe Palcic, as well as Jane Hoeppner and her three children, Allison, Amy and Drew. There was also a multimedia tribute.

"Hep was a special guy who had leadership qualities that not only impacted the football team, but the athletic department, the university and the community," said Miami athletic director Brad Bates. "And certainly at Hep's memorial service that day in Bloomington you saw that. If someone had shown up and looked at the number of people there, the first thing they would have said would have been 'I thought you said this guy was only here two years?' But Hep didn't require a lot of time to touch a great number of lives. The one thing I could tell the first time I met Terry Hoeppner was that he was a difference-maker."

After the service, the entire IU football team, in their game jerseys, formed a human tunnel on both sides of the road outside of Assembly Hall and lifted their helmets in unison as Hoeppner's hearse drove by en route to his burial. It was one final salute to a man whom they had come to know and love not just as a coach, but as a father figure for some, and a friend to everyone.

☆ ☆ ☆

As Terry Hoeppner stood at the podium, with the rose in the punch bowl on that December day in 2004, former IU All-American running back Anthony Thompson was one of those gathered for the press conference. He admitted later he wasn't sure what to make of Hoeppner that day. "He talked about how (the Rose Bowl) was the expectation and he was fired up," Thompson said. "And in my mind, I thought 'O.K. I don't really know him, but I want to see how long this lasts.'"

Looking back, with tears welling up in his eyes, Thompson was sure he knew the answer. "It was him," Thompson said. "I mean it was him until the day he died. Nothing changed from that time. And the people and culture took on his personality."

As a development officer for the IU Varsity Club, one of Thompson's jobs is to get IU coaches talking to donors. With Hoeppner it almost wasn't fair. Nobody could work a room like Terry Hoeppner.

"Coach Hep was a genius," Thompson said. "He would have donors wrapped in his hands. And Coach Hep did change the culture. It started with the football team, moved to the administration and throughout the Indiana University campus, and then spread like wildfire throughout the state."

IU president Adam Herbert seemed to sum up everyone's feelings with remarks he made the day that Hoeppner died. "We have lost a very strong, courageous, dedicated and visionary leader," Herbert said. "Coach Hep has done so much for Indiana University in far too short a time. Like all who knew him personally, I will miss his warmth and, above all, his friendship."

Chapter 2
"Hep-isms"

I t would be impossible to write a book about Terry Hoeppner without including his countless sayings. They were a part of everything he did, and he seemed to have one or more to fit any occasion.

They may have been sayings that were made famous by someone else, but if you knew Hep, you'd think he was the originator. And to be honest, any of the people who had the pleasure to know Hep will likely always credit him whenever one of those sayings comes to mind, or when shared with a loved one, colleague or friend.

His sayings were a big part of who he was. Sometimes he would credit Red Faught, his college coach at Franklin College. "Coach Faught used to say that 'tight end' was a condition, not a position," Hep once said during his weekly press conference, when someone asked why he didn't utilize the tight end more in his spread offense. At other times, when he thought his teams played well, but it wasn't reflected in the final score, he would use his familiar line, "It's not a judged competition."

Often he would just rattle something off and wait for a reaction. Every saying had special meaning, and with each one he had perfect delivery, as if he had said it a hundred times before. And he probably had. Hep was always trying to make his players and fellow coaches better men.

"He had all of these memorable sayings that were very profound when you really thought about them," said Miami of Ohio athletic director Brad Bates, Hep's boss for his final three seasons with the RedHawks. "Our students loved them and committed many of them to memory. They were very quick-hitting, and he was perpetually emphasizing them."

Bobby Johnson, who played at Miami of Ohio when Hep was an assistant coach there and later coached alongside him at both Miami and Indiana, said Hep's words were more than just football sayings. They were life lessons; lessons that sometimes took players a few years to grasp. But in many cases, former players still find themselves reciting a "Hep-ism" as a means to get through a challenging nonfootball situation.

The following are some of Hoeppner's favorite sayings, with commentary from some of the recipients of his words:

"Football is what I do. It's not who I am."

Indiana assistant coach Joe Palcic said Hoeppner first started saying that during the 2002 season at Miami, a year when Hep and his staff felt like the RedHawks were better than their 7-5 overall record and 5-3 conference mark indicated.

About midway through that season, following a bad loss, Hep was enjoying one of his favorite activities at home – soaking in the hot tub on his back deck. As he sat there, he was being really hard on himself for how he had handled a situation with his team. The more he thought about it, the more upset he got. After a while, he had worked himself up into a pretty good lather. Eventually, though, he got to the point where he took a step back and did a little self-examination. The next day he told his coaches in a staff meeting that the experience had changed him.

"I think as he thought about it he realized that football is what he does, but it's not who he is," Palcic said. "It wasn't going to define him as a man. It was just football, and I think after that he was a different person in how he approached some things."

IU assistant coach Matt Canada didn't have the daily history with Hoeppner that many of his fellow coaches did. Canada was on Gerry DiNardo's staff at Indiana and was one of three coaches Hoeppner retained when he was hired at IU in 2004. While many of the assistants had heard all of these sayings dozens of times before, Canada was experiencing it much in the same way as the players. He was hearing all of Hoeppner's words of wisdom for the first time.

Asked for his favorite "Hep-ism," Canada said he didn't think it was fair to Hep to single out just one or two. There were so many great ones that he had a hard time prioritizing them. But he did say the "Football is what I do" saying was one that hit home for him more than any other.

Canada has never made any bones about where his family ranks in his life. At Indiana football practices, it's an everyday occurrence to see Matt's wife and kids frolicking on the sidelines. And Canada wouldn't want it any other way. Simply put, if he's not doing something with football, he's with his family. And this was a kindred spirit he shared with Hoeppner, as well as with other members of the Indiana coaching staff. Hep always believed in giving football his all, but when the day was done he was looking forward to spending time with his wife Jane, his children and his grandchildren.

For Canada, Hep was the perfect role model. "My number one job is being a dad," Canada said. "Don't get me wrong. I love being a coach. I love my job. I'm very, very lucky and blessed. But that particular saying really hit home. And that's the way it should be. Football is important. It's how we feed our families. But it's a game. I get to be a kid. I get to sit around with 18-to-23 year olds and have fun.

"But that's the beauty of what Hep was all about. It's a game. Let's have fun. We don't have to be miserable. We don't have to be grumpy all the time. It's important, but we're lucky to get to do what we do."

Palcic heard Hep's favorite sayings over and over for the fifteen years they were together. But he never got tired of them. In fact, he loved seeing the gleam in Hoeppner's eyes when he recited one of his life lessons. And the "Football is what I do" saying was one of his favorites, too.

"I think that one hits home for me because this job can consume you," Palcic said. "You hear stories of different coaches who struggle. I think there's been a trend as a coach to be a grinder. You need to stay long hours and that kind of stuff. Hep showed me that you didn't have to do that. Family was definitely his first priority. Of course we have to get our work done, but when the work is done you go home and see your family."

"If you think you can, or you think you can't, you're right."

Indiana defensive lineman Greg Brown sat in meetings and heard Hep deliver those words, letting them sink in. He heard him say them many, many times, but they always seemed to make perfect sense. "I'd sit there and think about that every time he said it, and realized it was really true," Brown said. "If you say you can't do anything, you're not going to do it. But if you think you can, you at least have a chance."

Assistant coach George Ricomstrict was only with Hep for three seasons, one at Miami and two at Indiana, but that's the saying he'll use in the future as he grows as a coach. "That one just said it all, and it's something that should be easy for kids to grasp when you're trying to teach them life lessons," Ricomstrict said. "You don't have to make long speeches to teach. You just have to believe in what you're saying, and I know Hep really did."

"We don't have problems, we have opportunities."

When current IU football coach Bill Lynch thinks about Terry Hoeppner, this is the saying that comes to mind. The beauty of it is that Hep believed in it long before he got sick, but leaned on it even more after his first brain surgery.

"He coached that way and felt that way before he got sick," Lynch said. "But once he got sick, he never changed. And I think there are some people who think that's just something he used after he got sick, and that simply isn't the case.

I remember him saying the same thing when he was coaching at Franklin College and I was at Butler, thirty years ago."

"Have a plan. Work the plan. Plan for the unexpected."

Indiana wide receiver James Hardy learned many life lessons from Hoeppner. He loved all of his mentor's sayings, but there was one in particular that really hit home: "Have a plan. Work the plan. And plan for the unexpected."

"I was always the kind of person who tried to plan everything before it happened, and here comes Hep with that saying about planning for the unexpected, and that was something I had never done," Hardy said. "I always had negative thoughts, and I never planned for the unexpected because I always thought something bad was going to happen anyway.

"That was probably one of the best things he could have ever said to me because it definitely changed who I was and how I approached life. And it was obvious from the start that's how he lived his life, too. He came in here all amped up, and you just knew that he had a plan, and he was going to change some things.

He definitely had his plan and worked his plan, and that plan is still in place even after he's gone."

G.A.T.A.

One season when Hoeppner was at Miami, the defensive coaches had an inscription put on the back of their hats: "G.A.T.A." It was Hep's saying, and looking back, assistant coach Brian George said it epitomized Hoeppner's coaching philosophy. "It stood for Get After Their Ass," George said, "and that's what Hep's defensive teams always did. Hep was an intense guy, and he'd use any saying he could find to help motivate his troops. G.A.T.A. was one of those."

"Unexpected gifts at unexpected times pay huge dividends."

According to Bobby Johnson, this was family advice that Hep was always offering his young coaches, many of whom were newly married or just starting families. Hep had been there; he was experiencing grandchildren.

"What he meant was don't be afraid (or don't forget) at certain times to take the time to show your wife that she's important to you," Johnson said. "He would say, 'Yeah, she expects it on her birthday or on certain holidays, but what about that day that you just want to show her how much you love her?' There's no doubt that our women really support us in this profession.

"And I laugh at it now because I'm older and have kids. When I was younger, I'm not sure I quite got it. But now everything is perfectly clear. So every once in a while I'll stop and get flowers for no reason, and it's just my way of saying thanks to my wife for how much she supports me."

"Variety is the spice of life, except when it comes to your wife."

Former Indiana defensive lineman Russ Richardson laughed aloud when he thought about this one. Hoeppner would switch something around at practice, and he'd throw that one out there. The guys on the team who had steady girlfriends would always say to those who didn't, "Hey remember what Coach said: Variety is the spice of life, except when it comes to your wife."

"I remember one time he said that," Richardson said, "I looked at him and said, 'So the point of that is until you get married have as much fun as possible?' And Hep said, 'Yes sir.'"

"Every day is an interview."

Richardson said this one didn't completely sink in until after he had left IU and gone into the business world, but now that he's there, he uses it every single day. "It applies to any situation you're in," Richardson said. "You just never know who you're going to meet, and what possible impact they may have on your life."

Bobby Johnson was around Hoeppner as a player or coach for nearly seventeen years. As he looks back now, he often wishes he had taken more time to stop and smell the roses, another saying that if Hep didn't say, he was probably thinking.

"I now feel sometimes that I didn't take advantage of all his words," Johnson said. "I think, 'Boy, if I would have understood what he meant when he first said that, maybe I would have done this or maybe I would have handled that situation in another way.'"

"No job is too small."

Johnson remembers vividly a day at one of Hoeppner's summer camps when he and Joe Palcic were refereeing several 7-on-7 games. Before camp that day, Hoeppner held a brief meeting with his staff. He wanted them to remember that "No job is too small."

The saying kind of rolled off Johnson's back, and later he and Palcic were taking a break for a few minutes from refereeing.

"It was hot as hell, blistering hot, and we had something like seventy-five teams playing in a 7-on-7 tournament, and we had done a couple of games in a row," Johnson said. "We were getting a drink, and Joe and I were saying, 'Man, we've got two more games left. How are we going to get through this?'"

At about that time, the two looked over and saw Hoeppner walking around the sidelines scooping up trash and putting it into waste cans. The coach made eye contact with his assistants, and Johnson and Palcic looked at their feet.

"We looked at each other and said, 'What are we doing? There's the head coach over there walking around, picking up trash, and we're just sitting here.' And we realized he wasn't going to yell at us or anything, but we also flashed back to the meeting we had earlier in the day. No job was too small. Hep didn't only have the sayings, but he lived them, too. He wasn't one to waste his words. If he threw out one of his sayings, he had a reason for it."

"Don't be soft, but don't be stupid."

Players and coaches alike heard this one all the time as it related to football. Hoeppner himself, however, applied it to life on September 12, 2006, the night before he was scheduled to have his second brain surgery.

At a press conference in the IU football complex, Hep answered questions about the upcoming surgery. Someone asked him how long he thought it would be before he returned. "The guys will tell you because I tell them all the time, 'Don't be soft, but don't be stupid,'" Hoeppner said. "I've got to follow my advice there. I'm not going to lie around and go on vacation while the team's practicing and playing, but I'm not going to be stupid either."

"A lesser athlete would have fallen."

Billy Lynch admits he's a bit clumsy at times. But this saying surely wasn't reserved just for him. If someone tripped or stumbled on the field or perhaps in a hallway on the way to a meeting, Billy said the tendency was obviously to laugh. But Hep would say, "Hey, a lesser athlete would have fallen."

"He said that to me so many times. I'd always be stumbling or tripping up steps, and he'd say, 'Hey, a lesser athlete would have fallen.' It always made me feel a little bit better at an awkward moment."

"You have to know what kind of injury the athlete has, but you also have to know what kind of athlete the injury has."

Indiana defensive coordinator Brian George said this was one Hep used often to determine how tough certain players were. "Guys react differently to different injuries," George said. "Some guys, they break their fingernail and it's like they're dying. And Hep always understood that. We'd be looking at a training room report, and I'd say 'Well, this guy should be able to play.' But Hep would say, 'Maybe, but remember that's Johnny or whatever his name was, and Johnny doesn't come back from injuries real quickly.'

"And then he'd throw out his line: 'You have to know

what kind of injury the athlete has, but you also have to know what kind of athlete the injury has.'" George experiences this every day with his players, and the saying has taught him to look at every athlete a little bit differently.

"Life isn't always going to be fair."

This one hit home the most for Justin Frye, who played for Hoeppner at Indiana and later was a graduate assistant for the Hoosiers. In May of 2006, Frye lost his father to a brain tumor. A little over a year later, he lost his coach, too.

"Both my dad and Hep lived one motto to the fullest, that good, bad, ugly, you've got to keep on going," Frye said. "That's what I learned from Hep. Life isn't always going to be fair, and things aren't always going to be great. But you can't sit on your ass and mope about it. What do I need to do to make things better? What do I need to do to make it better for my family or my team? Any type of life situation applies."

"Don't Quit."

The "Don't Quit" poem always meant a lot to Hoeppner. He had the poem posted in the team room, and after he died it became a rallying cry for the 2007 IU football team. The words were printed on the back of the team's practice shirts as well as on game helmet decals.

"It's more than just two words. It's a motto that everyone should live by," said Indiana tackle Charlie Emerson. "There's no reason to quit. You need to keep going and persevere. Thick or thin, whatever your troubles are, there's always a light at the end of the tunnel. Whenever you think you're down, or you think you're at the end of the road, you're not. There's always hope and there's always something else out there for you."

Indiana running back Josiah Sears said he knew of the "Don't Quit" poem before coming to Indiana, but it was Hoeppner who made it come alive. "That's the way I was brought up," Sears said. "Even if something sucks, you stick it out and you keep working at it. If the end of the season comes and you don't want to do it anymore, that's one thing, but you never quit something in the middle. You always stick it out until the end.

"And Hep was all about that. It was the way he lived his life, and everyone on our football team knew that. When he wasn't doing well those last few months, we were aware of it, but we also knew that he was a fighter and would never quit. Whenever I look back on Hep, what I'll think about is how he never quit to the very end. No matter how difficult things got for him, he was in it for the long haul."

✮ ✮ ✮

It's impossible to put together a comprehensive list of Hep's sayings because every time it looked as if the list was complete, another one would come to mind. Or, in the course of an interview, someone else would throw out a favorite, and it wouldn't be one on the list. As you read these pages, you may remember one of your own. Here are some others:

"We need to be a thumb pointer and not a finger pointer."

"The more you do, the longer they will keep you around."

"Never take counsel of your fears."

"Once you know the truth, you are responsible for it."

"Set the bar high, then jump over it."

"Be in the right place at the right time."

"It's all in how you respond."

✮ ✮ ✮

Looking back on all those sayings, Bobby Johnson breaks into a satisfying smile. The day before Hep's memorial service at Assembly Hall in Bloomington, he and Indiana assistant coach Joe Palcic talked for hours about Hoeppner's sayings, as Palcic was preparing a speech to give at the service.

With some of them they laughed and others they cried, but inevitably they would come back to each other with "You know which one we forgot" or "I can't believe we didn't think of this one." But there were just so many, and they were all a part of what will be the legacy of Terry Hoeppner.

"When you look back on it from the perspective of 'Football is what I do, it's not who I am,' all of those sayings make sense," Johnson said. "I think what I'll take from all of this as I move forward in coaching is simply that football is a way to teach life lessons. And it's a way for us as coaches to help young men go where they can't take themselves, so that one day they'll be better men. Yeah, in the process you might make a better football player. But in the end, you really want to make a better person."

"Life isn't measured by the number of breaths you take, but by the number of breaths you take away."

IU athletic director Rick Greenspan said this was an old saying that he never heard Hep say, but one that fit his head coach to a "T." "He did take people's breaths away," Greenspan said. "He was a neat guy who loved life, and that came out in so many different ways."

Greenspan received countless letters from people who had never met Hoeppner but were inspired by one of his actions. He tells the story of a man who had cancer and was at his lowest moment before watching the IU-Wisconsin football game Hoeppner returned to coach just a few weeks after his second brain surgery in September of 2006.

"The letter said that he saw Hoeppner on TV, and he said to himself that if Terry Hoeppner can do that in those conditions, then he can get out of bed, too, and try to lead a productive life," Greenspan said. "I don't know if Hep ever realized how many people he touched that way, but I'm here to tell you that the number was great."

Don't Quit Poem

When things go wrong, as they sometimes will,
And the road you are trudging seems all up hill;
When the funds are low and the debts are high,
And you want to smile, but you have to sigh;
When care is pressing you down a bit
Rest if you must, but don't you quit.
For life is strange with its twists and turns,
As every one of us sometimes learns;
But many a coward turns about
When he might have won had he stuck it out.
But he learns too late when the night comes down
How close he was to the golden crown.
Victory is defeat turned inside out,
The silver tint of the clouds of doubt.
You will never know how near you are,
It may be close when it seems afar.
So stick to the fight when you are hardest hit
It's when things seem worst that you must not quit.

— Anonymous

Chapter 3
The Athletic Directors

Joel Maturi remembers the night in 1999 that Randy Walker made it official that he would be leaving Miami of Ohio to take the head coaching position at Northwestern. Maturi, the athletic director at Miami of Ohio at the time, knew Walker had been interviewing and realized there was a good chance he was going to accept the position. He recalls with crystal clarity the evening of January 20, 1999 when Walker called him with the news that he would be leaving for Northwestern.

Maturi was on his way to Kent State for a men's basketball game the night Walker called. A little while later, he got a second call from his secretary. She told him that the entire Miami of Ohio football team wanted to meet with him as soon as he returned from the game.

"I was riding on the team bus, and we weren't going to get back until 2:30 or 3 o'clock in the morning, so I said to her, 'Do they realize what time we're going to get back?' I'll never forget what she said. 'Oh they know exactly what time you'll be back, but they all want to be there to convince you to hire Terry Hoeppner as your next coach.'"

Maturi was able to put the team off until the next day, but he did meet with them as a group and listen to their ideas. The entire team was in agreement about Hoeppner. Hep had been an assistant at Miami for thirteen seasons and was a beloved figure. He was the ultimate player's coach. He loved Miami, was passionate about his vision for the program, and had paid his dues.

After listening to the players make their points, Maturi told them that Hoeppner would definitely be a strong candidate for the position, but he didn't want to make a knee jerk decision and just hire him without going through the interview process. He needed to look at all the candidates and hire the best. That wasn't a knock on Terry Hoeppner, but rather the responsible thing to do. He didn't think hiring Hep without going through the search process would be fair to Hoeppner or to Miami football.

So Maturi went ahead and interviewed a large pool of candidates.

"I'm not going to tell you who I interviewed, but some were names you would recognize," Maturi said. "I interviewed a lot of good people from the college football world. Some were assistants, some had been head coaches and some were current head coaches. It wasn't like I was drawing from a bad pool of candidates."

In the end, after an exhaustive process, he kept coming back to one name: Terry Hoeppner. "As much as Hep and Randy Walker got along, and they were great partners, you knew Terry wasn't Randy Walker, and I think the kids wanted a change," Maturi said. "They wanted a little different kind of leadership, and obviously Terry provided that. He was the perfect fit for Miami, and later for Indiana, without having the full opportunity there. I don't think there was anyone who fit what Indiana needed more than Terry Hoeppner."

Hoeppner spent six seasons as the head coach of the RedHawks. He had a winning record every year and in 2003 led Miami to a 13-1 record. That season, his team won the Mid-American Conference with an 8-0 record and won the GMAC Bowl. The RedHawks were ranked No. 10 in the nation in the final Associated Press poll, and as high as No. 11 in the BCS poll. The following season, Hoeppner's last at Miami, the RedHawks went 8-5 and played in the Independence Bowl.

✮ ✮ ✮

It was during a scouting trip to Shreveport, La., site of the Independence Bowl, that Brad Bates got the phone call he dreaded. Bates had taken over for Maturi as Miami's athletic director in 2002 when Maturi took the A.D. position at the University of Minnesota.

Bates wasn't a stranger to athletic directors calling him inquiring about Terry Hoeppner as a possible coach. After Miami's top ten finish in 2003, Hoeppner was a hot coach. Generally when those calls came, Hoeppner was flattered, but Bates knew his coach was loyal to Miami. There was only one school he worried about and that was Indiana. And IU had just fired Gerry DiNardo a week before.

When his phone rang, it was IU athletic director Rick Greenspan. Bates said at that moment he knew it was the beginning of the end of the Hoeppner era at Miami. "I think I even said to Rick on that call, 'Rick, he's going to be your guy. You're going to fall in love with him,'" Bates remembered. "But anyone who knew Terry could understand the way I was feeling about losing him, too. His passion, his energy and the way he ran his program were an athletic director's dream."

Greenspan had never met Terry Hoeppner. They spoke one time in a preliminary call a few days before, but most of his information came from others. A few years before that, when Greenspan was the athletic director at Army, Hoeppner's name had come up as a possible candidate at West Point, too. "I talked to some people I respected in football, and everybody told me that Hep was a hell of a guy and coach, and that he had paid his dues," Greenspan said. "But they also told me that he was a Midwestern guy, and they didn't think he'd come to Army."

When Greenspan was putting his list together of possible candidates at Indiana, he consulted associate athletic director Harold Mauro, whom he regarded as a walking encyclopedia of college football, especially in Indiana and the Midwest. Mauro was a linebacker at IU in 1964 and '65 and after a position switch, was the starting center on Indiana's

Rose Bowl team in 1967. He later served as an assistant coach at Northwestern for his college coach, John Pont, and eventually returned to IU as an assistant coach and as the Hoosiers' offensive coordinator in 1982 under head coach Lee Corso.

Mauro made a call to his old coach, John Pont, in Oxford, Ohio, home to Miami University. Pont, a former Miami head coach himself, frequently attended RedHawk football practices and was well-acquainted with Hoeppner. Mauro asked Pont if he could run over to practice and get Hoeppner's phone number, and then call him back. A few hours later, Mauro was able to deliver Hep's phone number to Greenspan.

A day or so later, Greenspan called Hoeppner. "It was what I would consider a typical conversation with Terry," Greenspan said. "You were excited and exhausted after it. I was so moved by the energy the guy had. Some people had questioned the fact that Hep was fifty-six or fifty-seven years old at the time, and whether he would have the energy to recruit and deal with all of the things I was going to need him to do to get this program back on its feet. And I remember coming out of that conversation thinking, 'Check that one off. That's not an issue.'"

In that first conversation, Greenspan shared a few of his ideas for Indiana and asked Hoeppner to share some of his own. He learned in that conversation about Hep's ties to the state of Indiana and his relationship with high school coaches. After that call, Greenspan was intrigued, but he didn't want to jump the gun until he had an opportunity to sit down with Hoeppner, look him in the eye and hear what he had to say. At the same time, that one phone call gave him a pretty good idea that he had found his new head football coach.

"His characteristics and background really hit at the core of what we were looking for," Greenspan said. "This was more than a job; it was something he really wanted. But you knew from talking to him that this situation had a chance to really be special."

The next day Greenspan called Brad Bates and told him he wanted to see about having a little more formal conversation with Hoeppner about the open Indiana job. Greenspan recalls Bates' response of 'Oh crap,' or something to that effect. When Greenspan asked what was wrong, Bates told him, "Oh, when you meet him you're just going to love him." Greenspan said, "It was almost as if Brad could see in his crystal ball that Hep would wind up being our next football coach."

Of course the rest is history. From the time Greenspan made that first phone call until Hep was introduced as the Indiana coach, a total of seven days had passed. During that time, Greenspan and Hoeppner met on two occasions, once at a motel in Franklin, Ind., and the other at a similar locale in Greensburg, Ind.

Greenspan shared the story of his first meeting with Hoeppner when he eulogized his head coach at Hep's memorial service in June of 2007. The meeting was at 2 p.m. on a Tuesday. Neither man knew what the other looked like, and so both consulted media guides as part of their homework.

After meeting in the parking lot, they walked into the registration area of the motel. Greenspan was carrying a briefcase, and Hep had a briefcase-like bag slung over his shoulder. "It was kind of a dreary December day, and there might have been four cars in the parking lot, and this 19-year-old clerk greets us," Greenspan said. "It probably had the appearance of some lewd relationship we were about to embark upon in this motel room. So I gave my name, he asked how many keys we needed, I told him just one, and he asked if we had any luggage, which we didn't."

Then the clerk asked how long they would be staying. "I told him we just needed the room for a couple of hours," Greenspan recalled with a smile. "I can only imagine what this kid was thinking. Looking back, I wasn't really thinking about appearances as much as I was just trying to find a quiet place where we could meet out of the way. This was a place that Hep suggested because he knew the area well. But I remember getting a funny look from this kid as we took our key and headed for that room."

☆ ☆ ☆

There was no denying that Miami's loss was about to be Indiana's gain. But as Brad Bates pointed out, the timing probably couldn't have been worse for Hoeppner. When Greenspan called and asked Bates' permission that day, Hoeppner and Bates were together in Shreveport, La. Just a few days before that, the Independence Bowl had announced that Miami of Ohio would face Iowa State in the annual bowl game on December 28. Bates and Hep were checking out where the team would stay and all the other logistics for the game.

"It was tough for Terry because he absolutely loved Miami, had been there for so long, and we were still in the season and preparing for a bowl game," Bates said. "So he had all of these emotions tied to Miami, but at the same time he grew up in Indiana, was a Hoosier from the beginning, and loved IU from his earliest recollection. If there was any place he would ever consider going, this was it."

After Hoeppner told Greenspan he would take the Indiana job, Greenspan asked him what his thoughts were about coaching Miami in the Independence Bowl twelve days after being introduced as the new IU coach. Hoeppner told him he couldn't wait to get started at Indiana, but also felt that he really needed to coach the RedHawks in the bowl game. Then he turned the question back to Greenspan and asked the IU A.D. what he thought.

"I told him I would have been disappointed if he had given me any other answer," Greenspan said. "He worked with those kids for three or four years, had gone with them through the season, and while every school views things differently, how you enter a place and how you leave make lasting impressions. I told him the place he needed to be in late December was coaching Miami in the Independence Bowl."

Hoeppner did just that. Unfortunately, his final game at Miami was a 17-13 Independence Bowl loss to Iowa State. It was a game where the television ratings in Indiana had to have been particularly high.

✬ ✬ ✬

Bates and Hoeppner were together about two-and-a-half years, about the same amount of time Hoeppner was at Indiana. Bates came on board midway through the 2002 football season and was there when Hep left for Indiana in December of 2004.

When Bates was interviewing for the Miami A.D. job, he did a little investigating of the coaches with whom he might be working. The weekend of his first interview, Miami had a football game with Cincinnati. Bates was at Vanderbilt at the time and, without a home game that weekend, was able to drive to the game and blend into the crowd to observe Hoeppner from afar.

"I had a firsthand opportunity to kind of study him and see his demeanor on the sideline, his passion and all the rest," Bates said. "After the game we flipped on the radio and listened to his postgame show. I was fascinated by his energy and his enthusiasm. Miami won the game, so obviously he was a little more excited than he would have been if they had gotten beat, but there was such an engaging quality to him, even over the radio. To this day I can still remember exactly what they were talking about."

After Bates got the job, his relationship with Hoeppner began to blossom. "We were squarely locked, arm in arm," Bates said. "The head football coach is in a critical leadership position. To be on the same page with him and share the same philosophy are very important. The way you approach student-athlete development, the drive to engage fans, to perpetually invite back alumni, those are all really important parts of the job.

"Terry and I had a great relationship, and my sense is that Terry and Rick (Greenspan) had that same relationship, too. Terry was a good friend. He was a really good guy, somebody you wanted to be around. Not just professionally, but personally."

Like everyone who knew Hep, Bates has many fond memories of his friend. One of his favorites involved both Brad and his wife, Michelle. When they first moved to Miami, the Bates lived in a 107-year-old house on campus. One year, Hoeppner and Bates were about to drive to Detroit for the Mid-American Conference coaches meetings where Brad had a speaking engagement. The two men were running late. About fifteen minutes before Hoeppner arrived at the house, the Bates' discovered a bat in their house.

"As you can imagine, my wife wasn't real excited about having that bat in the house," Bates said. "So I was thinking we could just call somebody over to take care of it because Terry and I needed to get going. As it was, we weren't going to get to Detroit before midnight, and the meetings started at 8:00 the next morning."

Not surprisingly, Hep had a different idea. From the moment he heard about the bat, he was making his plan, working his plan and even planning for the unexpected. He wanted to know where the sheets and blankets were that they could throw over the bat. He was blocking off doorways so the bat could be cornered into one room. "And sure enough, in about fifteen minutes we were able to capture the bat and put it in a cage. I think Michelle turned it over to the Humane Society or something."

Bates said that story revealed something about Hoeppner. Simply put, he was a friend above all else. "He has so many things on his plate, yet here he is taking time to help a woman who is very anxious," Bates said. "That's the leader in him. Immediately he starts figuring out how we're going to fix the situation. In this case, how we're going to get the bat. But there are so many examples of him taking charge in so many different areas. That's part of what made him such a great guy."

☆ ☆ ☆

When Maturi heard that Hoeppner was leaving Miami for Indiana, he thought "Good for Hep." Maturi loved Miami just like Hoeppner, but he also understood what it meant for Hep to land his dream job. And he always wanted what was best for his friend.

Maturi had much the same feelings about Minnesota when he left Miami to become the athletic director at the University of Minnesota in 2002. His roots were in Minnesota, like Hep's in the Hoosier State.

"I told the president when I was hired at Miami that I'm at the stage of my career where I may have one stop left," Maturi said. "I wasn't looking, but if it were Wisconsin, where I spent ten years of my life, or Notre Dame, which was my alma mater, or Minnesota that came calling, I would have to consider it." It was the same thing for Hoeppner when Indiana came calling. As much as he loved Miami, it was simply an offer he couldn't refuse.

"A Big Ten school provides you with the highest stage in your profession," Maturi said. "I think many of us wonder if our philosophies and our way of doing things can survive at that BCS level, and I think Terry always wondered that as well."

Because Hoeppner was an assistant coach when Maturi got the job at Miami, he and the athletic director had a different kind of relationship. Maturi said they were friends long before they were working partners.

"I treasured Terry Hoeppner as a coach and a friend," Maturi said. "I was an educator first. I spent twenty years as a high school coach. In my career, I've been blessed to be around a lot of great coaches, but I've never been with anybody who shared the value of education and really cared about college athletics more than Terry Hoeppner.

"As competitive as he was, he truly cared about the welfare and best interests of the kids. Sometimes that meant sitting players who might have helped him win on a Saturday. Sometimes it made for some tough losses. I know that since he's no longer with us it may sound trite, but I'm speaking from the heart."

Maturi's relationship with Hep was non-football first and football second. "We had some great discussions about being educators that were important to both of us," Maturi said. "We didn't talk about X's and O's. We'd talk about the impact that we could have on young people's lives."

☆ ☆ ☆

As soon as Greenspan had his man, he began talking about the "partnership" he had with his new head coach. "We had a unique relationship from the start because I knew there were going to be things I'd call on him to do that maybe other coaches in the Big Ten felt were beneath them," Greenspan said. "Some coaches might have resented being out on the front lines hustling tickets and talking to people about the program. Maybe that was what you did at a Division I-AA school, but not at a place like Indiana.

"So I tried to relay that I needed a partner. If we needed to jump in the car and go see 150 people in Columbus, Indiana, I needed someone who was going to say, 'Hey, what time are we leaving?' And Terry's personality was a great fit in that aspect."

When Greenspan offered Hoeppner the job, he didn't take long to call back with an acceptance. From there, things moved pretty quickly. On December 16, Greenspan and his wife Jenny boarded a small plane headed for Oxford to pick up the Hoeppners for the Indiana press conference, where he would be named the new IU coach. The flight took fifteen minutes. Upon landing at Bloomington airport, the Indiana State Police detail, headed by Curt Durnil and his father Jim, met the plane and escorted them to Bryan Hall, where they met IU president Adam Herbert. There, Greenspan, Hoeppner and Herbert made it official by signing the contract, which would pay the new coach just over $600,000 per season.

Herbert was impressed with the police escort Hoeppner received, and even commented that "not even the governor gets an escort like that." Hep was quick with his reply: "Well,

I guess the governor hasn't won forty-eight games."

A few hours later, Hep was introduced at the press con-ference and stood at the podium with the rose in the punch bowl. Greenspan admitted later that the punch bowl was far from a premeditated idea. In fact, he came up with it just a few hours before the press conference. A lot of people were under the impression the bowl was an actual trophy the Hoosiers had received for their participation in the Rose Bowl. Greenspan made it clear that was not the case.

"Oh no, that was just a bowl from the catering kitchen or somewhere," Greenspan said. "I had this last-minute idea and I asked my secretary, Terri Smithson, to see if she could find some kind of ceramic bowl or something, and that was what she came back with. The same with the rose. Someone probably ran up to a florist or a grocery store. It wasn't some grand scheme."

Later that day, Greenspan got his first glimpse into the kind of coach Hoeppner would be for the university. The press conference happened to fall on a day when Greenspan had invited the entire athletic department out to his house for a get-together. The event was catered, with about 150 people on the guest list, and Jenny Greenspan had to leave the press conference as soon as it was over to get home and take care of last-minute details.

Because of the press conference, Hoeppner had pushed his practice back at Miami, where the RedHawks continued preparations for the Independence Bowl. Greenspan told him after the press conference that he knew Hep had to run, but he would be in touch every day until after his season had officially ended. When Greenspan told Hoeppner why he needed to make a hasty exit after the press conference, Hep said, "I've still got a little time. Why don't I come by?"

So Hoeppner, in an Indiana State Police car, followed Greenspan back to his home, which is a good twenty min-utes from the athletic complex. Upon arriving, he assumed the role of greeter. As each person came in, Hep introduced himself, "Hi, I'm Terry Hoeppner. I'm your new football coach." That experience really left a great first impression on Greenspan and his staff. "It made Hep that much more approachable in everyone's eyes."

A new chapter of IU football was about to begin.

✮ ✮ ✮

Greenspan has a number of personal Hoeppner memories. Two of his favorites are of time spent on the A.D.'s pontoon boat on Lake Monroe, outside of Bloomington.

One Sunday afternoon he and his wife Jenny were out on the pontoon when Hep called him on his cell phone. The coach wanted to know what Greenspan was up to, and the A.D. said they were just hoisting a cold beverage or two and listening to the Yankee game on XM Radio. Hep then proceeded to invite himself over. He and Jane wanted to know if they could meet with them in an hour or so. He was probably twenty minutes away and said they would get cleaned up and head out. "I said, 'Sure, coach, we'll see you then,'" Greenspan recalled.

Five minutes later, Hoeppner came flying up on a jet ski, did a quick turn, and sent water flying in all directions. He had his cell phone in hand. "Gotcha, didn't I?" Greenspan, with a laugh, recalls Hep saying. "He had been floating around on the water with his family and came by to mess with us a little bit."

Another day in the summer of 2006, sometime after Hoeppner's first brain surgery, Greenspan had probably eight people on the pontoon. It was a weekend, and they had two big coolers full of beer and champagne, and a host of sandwiches, and they were spending a relaxing day on the lake.

"I was driving the boat, which I'm rarely allowed to do, and there were a bunch of people on speed boats making big wakes," Greenspan said. "Well, we hit a wake wrong, and the nose went down, sending these two huge coolers full of stuff into the water. I turned around to look at the situation with my palms in the air, and everyone just looked at each other."

Everyone, that is, but Hep. He ripped off his shirt and dived in. He went down after these two sinking coolers, and when he came back up he had a two-liter bottle of Mountain Dew and a two-liter of Coke in his hands, the only items that didn't sink. "As long as I can remember, I still gave him crap about his heroic effort to save the soda when the beer and champagne and all the good stuff sank," Greenspan said.

One other memory was on New Year's Eve in 2006 at a party hosted by John Mellencamp. At midnight, Mellencamp came out to play with his band, and the Greenspans and Hoeppners were standing together off to one side. Some people were dancing, but most were just standing there listening to the music. Hoeppner decided that wasn't right and asked, "Does anybody know how to do the Electric Slide?"

"That was his favorite dance, and within five minutes he had everybody doing whatever the Electric Slide is. It was a typical Hep moment," Greenspan said. "He just had that charismatic way of engaging people."

☆ ☆ ☆

Until the day Hep died, Greenspan had become a believer that some way, somehow, Hoeppner was going to find a way to beat brain cancer. He had fallen to the depths, but he was going to bounce back. His family believed it, and right up until the end they expected him to open his eyes and start getting better. And more importantly, Hep himself believed it.

"Terry had overcome so much, to the point where if he said something was going to happen, it did," Greenspan said. "He would say things like, 'You tell me I can't make people care about Indiana football? I'm going to make people care.' Or, 'You tell me I can't make it back from surgery early? I'm going to make it back earlier than anyone expected.' And that's the way he lived his life, which defines inspiration."

Chapter 4
Bill Lynch

Shortly after Terry Hoeppner was named Indiana's head football coach in December of 2004, he began assembling his entire staff, with one exception. He left open the assistant head coach position because he didn't want to rush the hire. He knew who his first choice was, but he wanted to go about making contact the right way.

Billy Lynch Jr. was an assistant coach with Hoeppner at Miami and was one of the coaches Hep brought along with him to Indiana. In mid-January, Lynch was out recruiting at Noblesville High School when he saw that he had a missed call on his cell phone. It was Hep. He walked outside and dialed Hep's number to see what was up. Hoeppner told him he had an idea.

"What do you think about your dad as assistant head coach/offensive coordinator at Indiana?" Hoeppner asked. Billy was excited. "Wow, that sounds like a great idea," he said.

Billy had played for his dad at Ball State, and the thought of coaching with him in the Big Ten was like a dream come true. As he sat in his car in the Noblesville parking lot, Billy continued to talk with Hep about what his coach wanted him to do next. First Hep wanted to know if Billy thought that his dad would take the job. He knew it would be hard for Bill Sr. to leave DePauw, where he was head coach of his own program again, but he hoped that the lure of coaching at IU would be enough to get him to come.

Hoeppner then told him he had just one recruit left to get. Billy played along, "Who's that, my dad?" "No," Hoeppner said. "Your mom." Hoeppner told Billy that he wanted him to drive to Muncie right then and get to work on Linda Lynch. "Hep, knowing my mom and dad for so long, knew that my mom had to be sold, not my dad," Billy Lynch said. "I do know that after my dad and Hep talked about the job a lot, at some point, as Hep had done with practically everybody else in the state of Indiana, he sold him on the vision of what we could do here. I know that my dad was very happy at DePauw, and it was tough for him to leave, but Hep has a way about him, and he convinced him that it was the right thing to do."

Billy had his dad pegged on this one. The man who was the head coach at Ball State from 1995-2002 had found himself at home in Greencastle, Ind. at DePauw. In his first season in 2004, DePauw went 8-2 and Lynch was the conference's coach of the year.

"I'm sure to Billy the whole thing was a no-brainer, but Terry knew that you get to a certain age and things are different," Lynch said. "I had a pretty good job. It certainly wasn't the Big Ten, and it wasn't working with him, but it was a good situation. You think of security and all of that, and it was a good place for me. So Hep knew it wasn't just going to be one phone call and that would be that. But as soon as he did call, I knew that it was going to be pretty hard to turn him down."

Lynch had worked at Indiana once before, as an assistant coach under Bill Mallory in 1993 and '94. In fact, he coached on the last Indiana team to make it to a bowl game. The '93 Hoosiers went 8-3 in the regular season before losing to Virginia Tech in the Independence Bowl.

"Part of it was the attraction of coming to Indiana because I had coached here before," Lynch said. "I liked it here and knew you could win here. It would take a lot of work, but it could be done. And my respect for Hep and our friendship, and never really having had the chance to work with him, I thought that would be fun. So it didn't take too long to make up my mind."

Lynch and Hoeppner had played against each other forever. When Lynch was an assistant at Butler, Hoeppner was an assistant at Franklin College. When Lynch was at Ball State, Hoeppner was at Miami of Ohio. They had become good friends nearly thirty years ago in the coaching clinics circuit and enjoyed competing against each other – Hoeppner's defense versus Lynch's offense.

But now that they were finally united on the same team, Lynch was excited. "It was fun because Hep never changed," Lynch said. "It wasn't like there was the Terry Hoeppner I knew almost thirty years ago, and then all of sudden he was a different guy. He had different responsibilities, a different role, but it was still that same enthusiasm and optimism and "Let's go" kind of attitude.

"He still had all of his sayings and quotes. He lived them. That's what was unique about him. Hep didn't have a public side and a private side. That was Terry Hoeppner. So it was fun to be around him and coach with him. We had been through a lot of the same battles over the years, and I guess I would say that we knew what we were getting ourselves into."

Perhaps Lynch knew what he was getting himself into coaching with Hoeppner, but he couldn't have known what his life and his role with the Hoosiers would be like twenty-nine months after he took the job. Three games into the 2006 season, Lynch filled in for Hoeppner as IU's head coach when his boss had his second brain surgery. Six months later, he took over for Hep in spring football when Hoeppner needed some time to rest and re-energize. Later, he was named interim coach for the 2007 season. A few days after that announcement, the interim title was removed when his close friend died from brain cancer complications.

It was a bittersweet moment for Lynch. With Indiana football in his blood, Lynch was honored to be the head coach. But he never wanted it to be this way. He never wanted it to be because Hep had passed on. Because Lynch headed the program in the spring and into the summer, he had some time to prepare himself. But losing Hep was still one of the most difficult things he had ever had to go through.

"One of the things that got me through it was thinking about the way Hep would want me to proceed," Lynch said. "Hep would want me to get all the coaches and players on the same page and get their minds on playing football. I think all of us will always carry a piece of Terry Hoeppner with us. He was that kind of guy."

☆ ☆ ☆

Bill Lynch and Terry Hoeppner first started competing against each other in 1980. Lynch was the offensive coordinator at his alma mater, Butler, and Hoeppner was the defensive coordinator at his alma mater, Franklin. For the next four seasons, Lynch and Hoeppner went toe to toe. "His teams were hard to play against," Lynch said. "There were a couple of years when trying to get a first down was hard, let alone beating them."

Even back then, Hoeppner was innovative. He was always passionate about his profession and was eager to sell Lynch on the latest and greatest new idea. The two coaches had become good friends, and even though they weren't at the same school, they would talk a lot in the offseason and share ideas.

"Hep was always an idea guy," Lynch said. "Years ago, when we were both assistant coaches, we'd run into each other at a clinic or visiting some other spring practice, and he'd say 'Hey, I saw this. This is going to work. This is great!' It might be a scheme or an approach to recruiting or any number of other things. But he was always that kind of guy. When he got an idea and believed in it, he sold it."

Lynch got to the point where he looked forward to those chance meetings. If he hadn't seen Hep in a few months, he knew that when they got together Hoeppner was going to have something new for him. And it wasn't always just defensive football. There were times when he'd pull Lynch off to the side with an offensive idea, too.

"I remember him saying, 'I saw this play run and it is really hard to defend. You should put that play in your offense,'" Lynch said. "He didn't care that we might be competing against each other next season; he just loved to share his ideas. And I remember walking away a few times thinking that I should probably try it. I figured if he believed in it that strongly, there must be something to it."

One of Lynch's funniest memories of Hoeppner came from those early years at Franklin and Butler and involved the headphones that coaches used to talk with each other during the games. "Back then it certainly wasn't high tech," Lynch said. "Headphones were like having a rotary dial to talk to your coach. And the press boxes were pretty close to the field. In fact, you could just about turn around and yell up to the press box if you wanted to. It was that close to the field."

Butler's Bill Sylvester and Franklin's Red Faught were the football coaches at that time and were both well-respected in their communities. Any time they faced off, the game turned into a war. In one game between the two teams Butler employed a new state-of-the-art battery-operated headphone. They didn't work that well back then. Franklin had the more conventional headsets. It was the rule then, and it still is in many places today, that if one side's headsets go out, the other side has to take theirs off, too.

"At some point in the game, Hep got really mad and threw his headset down and broke it," Lynch remembered. "He walked over to Red Faught and told him what had happened. Red told him that he was going to have to cross the field and tell Sylvester to take his off, too.

"So right in the middle of the game, there's a timeout, and Hep had to run across the middle of the field and tell our head coach we had to take our headsets off, too, because of something he had done. All I remember is Coach Sylvester looking at him and saying, 'What in the hell are you talking about?' And Hep just stood there embarrassed as the coaches watched from the press box. While we felt for him, it was pretty funny, too. Hep and I revisited that story many times over the years."

★ ★ ★

Lynch finds it interesting the way that people remember Terry Hoeppner. Everyone remembers his passion, his enthusiasm and his salesmanship on a variety of different levels. When others think of him, they think of the traditions he started at Indiana, including "The Rock" and "The Walk to the Rock." Still others talk about what a great family guy he was.

And while Lynch believes all those things are true, he said there's another way to remember Hoeppner that some people sometimes forget – He was a great football coach. "All the enthusiasm and all of the things he brought to this place are true, but he was a great football coach," Lynch said. "He was a really good X's and O's guy. A really good practice guy. A good game day guy. He was just a really good football coach.

"Sometimes I think people relate more to his personality than they do to his football skills. My regret is that Hep didn't get to stay long enough to prove what a great football coach he really was. Because there's a whole lot of guys out there who worked with him and coached against him, who will tell you that playing against his teams was really tough. He was just a great ball coach."

★ ★ ★

Heading into the 2007 season, Bill Lynch's task was to keep the Indiana players focused and try to find a way to achieve Hoeppner's goal of playing thirteen games. Billy Lynch, IU's wide receivers coach and son of the Hoosier head coach, said he knows his dad will be fine, but he also feels for him.

50

"He's in a tough spot obviously, because he and Hep were such good friends," Billy Lynch said. "I think it's a totally different situation than if he came in working for a guy he never met. But they had so much history and so much respect for each other; I think he'll be coaching with a heavy heart. Inside the lines I don't think it will be too much of an issue because my dad has done all of that before. But it's all of the other stuff that is going to be hard."

Lynch is going to take it one day at a time and do his best to honor the memory of his friend. "Terry laid a great foundation here in a short time, and these players are really looking forward to putting it all on the line for Hep in 2007," Lynch said. "Our job is to continue what he started and to realize some of the visions he had for this program."

Chapter 5
Family First

You could never say Terry Hoeppner didn't have his priorities in the right place. Football was what he did, but it wasn't who he was.

He *was* a family man. He *was* a great husband to Jane, his devoted wife of thirty-nine years. He *was* an incredible father to Amy, Allison and Drew. He *was* a loving grandfather to Tucker, Spencer, Tate and Quinn.

He *was* a proud son who often talked about how blessed he was that his mother, Phyllis, was still alive to see him coaching at Indiana. He *was* a good brother to Pam and Mark.

He *was* a father figure, a role model and a friend to the hundreds of players he coached and the numerous assistant coaches who worked at his side.

Most of all, he *was* a man who believed that family should always come first.

★ ★ ★

Terry and Jane Hoeppner had something special. You could tell by the way they looked at each other. It was in the stories they told. The way that one would start to say something and the other, right on cue, would finish the sentence. They were of one mind, body and spirit.

With Hep, all you had to see was the way he looked at his wife and listen to the things he said about her when she left the room. "Isn't she something?" Hoeppner said on many occasions to coaches, friends and family members. "I've got to be the luckiest man alive to have the love of a woman like that."

Long time Indiana University football and basketball broadcaster Don Fischer said the Hoeppners took love to a different level. Though he was around them quite a bit in the two-and-a-half years that Hep was at IU, he never heard them so much as raise their voice at one another. "I wonder if they ever had a fight?" Fischer asked.

"If I could treat my wife half as good as he treated Jane, or if my wife thought I'm half as special as Jane thinks Terry is, that would be about as good as it gets," Fischer said. "Their relationship was unique. I've never seen any couple closer. They always seemed to be on the same page."

Anthony Thompson, the former Indiana All-American running back, was one of Hoeppner's ministers the last eighteen months of his life. You always hear the old cliché that behind every good man is a good woman. In the case of Jane Hoeppner, though, Thompson had to disagree. He said Jane was side-by-side with her husband through the good times and the bad.

"The last eighteen months of his life, she was always there," Thompson said. "She wouldn't leave the house. She wouldn't do anything. And Hep loved to brag about her. She would leave the room and he'd lean over to me and whisper, 'A.T., that woman is amazing!' I learned some things about true love from seeing Terry and Jane Hoeppner together."

The phrase "in sickness and in health" embodied the Hoeppner's relationship. Before Hep got sick, Jane seemed like she was always there. After he got sick, she *was* always there. She was at every practice, every training table dinner. If you saw Hep without Jane, there was a pretty good chance she'd be stepping around the corner any moment.

Every weekly press conference, Jane was always at a table in the back of the room, rolling her eyes at some of the things her husband said. And he had fun with it, too. He loved to refer to her as his able-bodied assistant, or his nurse, or as his associate head coach. But she was there because she wanted to be there, and it was obvious that there was no place that Hep would rather she be.

★ ★ ★

Before Hep got sick, there were times they'd be apart, but rarely for very long. Sure, they did some things independently, like if Terry was on a recruiting trip or had a speaking engagement, but if they could be together they were.

Brian George said recruiting trips were more of an issue at Miami because he and his fellow assistants did the job by driving around the Midwest. When it came time in January to "seal the deal" with some of the recruits and bring in the head coach, Hep would often be on the road for a week or more. One coach would drive him for a day or so, then make an exchange with another coach, who'd pick Hep up and drive him to that coach's recruiting area.

"The assistant coaches would fight to have him at the beginning of the week and not the end," George said. "He'd be miserable by the end of the week. And it was because he wasn't around Jane. A whole week without Jane, and you could bet Hep was going to be a grump. And he was a real grump. It didn't matter what you did, it was wrong."

George said the coaches had a routine that helped during those times. They always tried to find a bookstore, because Hoeppner loved to read. Picking a hotel that had a workout room and a whirlpool was big, too.

"He loved to get up and work out in the morning, although it wasn't really a workout," George said. "He went down to the weight room and did a couple of curls, then jumped in the swimming pool and floated around, and finally settled into the hot tub. But he loved to have his morning for that. So you always had to make sure that Coach was taken care of, or you were in big trouble."

George remembers one season when he had to take on some extra recruiting responsibilities. On a driving trip during recruiting season he had to take Hoeppner from Oxford to Pittsburgh, then on to Detroit, Grand Rapids, and back to Oxford. As George can attest, it was a long time to be in the car with Hep.

"It was quite a trip," George said, laughing out loud. "We went to the mall to find a bookstore. I made sure the hotel had a pool and a workout room. And I got him a suite. But by the end of the week, he was his old grumpy self. It just tells you a lot about how much he loved his wife. We finally got to the point where we started taking Jane with us on some of those trips, especially after we came to Indiana and were flying more."

But through it all, the coaches learned a lot about devotion to their own families. Hoeppner's 'Family First' philosophy couldn't help but rub off on those around him. "He taught me a lot just by the way he treated his wife," said IU assistant coach Matt Canada. "He wanted to be with her all the time, and you can't fake that. You could see that it was genuine, and it was very refreshing."

Assistant coach Joe Palcic, who spent fifteen years with Hoeppner as either a player or a coach, always thought Terry and Jane had an incredible marriage, but in the last two years they seemed to get even closer. "I didn't think that was possible, but Jane told me a couple of different times that their relationship had gotten even stronger since he came to Indiana," Palcic said. "The thing I've learned from them is to cherish the quality time you have with your wife, so you never have any regrets later."

☆ ☆ ☆

On the day his dad died, Drew Hoeppner sat in his basement with a reporter and recalled loving memories. But even though it had only been a few hours since his father had passed away, Drew was already focusing his attention on the one person who was going to miss him more than anyone else.

"He's fine. He's in a better place. His hip doesn't hurt anymore," Drew Hoeppner said. "But you've seen how close they are. Her best friend is gone. Her soul mate. And that's what the hardest part is for me because I'm a self-declared mama's boy, and I'm not ashamed of that. But I hate to see her hurt. That's the hardest part in all of this."

Drew was reminded of the fact that when people look at the Hoeppner family, they see more than one "rock." Sure, Terry and his "Don't Quit" persona were front and center, but Jane more than held her own in that department. "Oh, she's strong. There's no doubt about that," Drew Hoeppner said that day. "She's just sad. We all are. We miss him. We weren't done."

☆ ☆ ☆

Hoeppner was the typical proud papa when it came to his children. He bragged about how his son and two daughters had all received their degrees from Miami of Ohio. He talked about how proud he was that his two girls had married two good guys and were doing a great job raising their boys. He beamed about the fact that his son Drew was studying to become a pilot, and Drew was equally proud a few days before his dad died to be able to tell him that he had just accepted a job with U.S. Airways Express and would soon be flying commercial.

Don Fischer was quite impressed with the Hoeppner family unit. The first season Hoeppner was at Indiana, Hep invited Fischer and his wife Susy to his home after every home game for a gathering with family members. And it was truly a family time. Allison and Amy were there with their husbands and kids. Drew was there, too. His mother was there, as well as some family members from Hep's hometown of Woodburn, Ind. Sometimes there was family from Jane's side as well.

"He made me out to be a rock star in his house," Fischer said. "He'd tell me, 'Man, Fish, my entire family is so excited that you're going to be there today,' things like that. Yet I loved every minute of it because of how engaging he was with me and Susy. And Jane was the same way. They made us feel like we were part of their home. They made us feel like family."

One of the things Fischer remembered from those gatherings is that the entire family would watch the replay of that day's game on the big screen television in the basement. They were all screaming and yelling at the TV, almost as if they were watching the game live.

"They responded like that to every play," Fischer said. "If someone didn't make a play, they'd grumble about it. If an official made a bad call, they'd be all over him. Or if they made a play, they'd be screaming at the top of their lungs."

And right in the middle of them sat Terry Hoeppner, not saying a word. Fischer said he had a little grin on his face that seemed to say, "This is great, isn't it?" "The sense you got was that he absolutely loved having his family around him sharing those moments together," Fischer said. "It was really special. I can't think of another way to describe it. Those were special times."

Bobby Johnson, who played for Hoeppner at Miami and later coached with him both at Miami and Indiana, has a fond memory of Hep's daughter, Amy. Hoeppner had a weekly radio show at a local restaurant in Oxford, and when practice ended, all the assistants hustled over to the restaurant because it was a chance to eat with their families and also listen to the show.

One of the reasons to listen was a frequent female caller who seemed very knowledgeable about Miami football. The staff was well aware it was Hep's daughter, Amy, who would call the show and disguise her voice every week to ask her dad a question.

"She'd call every week using a false name and ask a question to kind of lead him into a topic that he told her ahead of time he wanted to talk about," Johnson said. "It was a riot. So we'd go up there and eat and wait for Amy to call and laugh about whatever name she would use that week."

✮ ✮ ✮

There was no question that family was always at the top of Hoeppner's list, but it extended beyond just his immediate family. He considered his coaches family, and the same was true of their wives and children. One of the basic principles he tried to convey to his coaches was making sure they understood where family should rank in their lives. At first, his assistants marveled at how Hep bent over backward to make sure that wives and children were a visible part of his football program.

"I don't care if it was the Homecoming parade or Sunday afternoon practices or any one of a dozen other things, Terry would always say, 'I've got to bring the grandkids,'" recalled Joel Maturi, Hep's athletic director at Miami. "He was so family-oriented in everything he did. I think that, more than anything, revealed a lot about the person Terry Hoeppner was."

Shane Montgomery, who was on Hep's staff at Miami and later took his place as head coach, said Hoeppner's approach to family mirrored the way Montgomery was brought up, making it easy for him to embrace the principles. "With some head coaches, you get to where you hate to go to work," Montgomery said. "You're expected to be in the office all night. With Hep it wasn't that way. You truly enjoyed coming to work every day. He wanted you to spend time with your family. It was possible to balance work, family and your friends."

Assistant coach Brian George said Hep's complete devotion to family was rare in their profession. "He was so close to his family, and I think that's something that is lost in this business sometimes," George said. "The families in a lot of Division I or NFL coaching staffs are excluded from a lot. But Hep always brought them in instead of pushing them away."

And it wasn't just for show either. It was a commitment from the head coach to his assistants, and he wanted to make sure that his guys never lost sight of what was truly important in life. If you came to an Indiana football practice either of his two seasons in Bloomington, you might have seen Hep sitting after practice in a golf cart with Jane right by his side. But you'd also see his toddler grandson Quinn (he called him Quinny) climbing all over "Pa" as well. Quinn loved his toy John Deere tractors, and you could be certain that his front loader would be digging into the practice field turf. Hep would just watch and smile.

But it wasn't just Quinn or his brother Tate, or Tucker and Spencer down with their mom and dad from Cincinnati. No, this wasn't reserved just for the four grandchildren. There were kids everywhere. Coach's kids wrapped up in their own little world. Some might be rolling around on the blocking pads or playing with any number of IU football players who had stopped to talk with them as they headed to the locker room. They were there because Hoeppner believed it was important that football and families mixed. He wouldn't have it any other way.

Michelle Canada, wife of Indiana assistant coach Matt Canada, credits both Terry and Jane Hoeppner with having a profound impact on her family life. The Canada's children, Victoria and Chris, were fixtures at weekly practice in Bloomington.

"He gave the guys the privilege of being fathers," Michelle Canada said. "He also was a role model. It's a great lesson for all of us. Hep showed the men how to be good husbands, and Jane showed the women how to be good wives. They were an incredible team, and we all were the benefactors."

What Hoeppner afforded his staff was far from the norm in college football. In most programs, the first day of August signals a four- or five-month period where the family shouldn't count on dad too much. Sixteen-hour days become the norm. Coaches get home after the kids go to bed, and they either leave before the kids get up, or they try to catch up on some much needed sleep in the early morning hours. It simply becomes a way of life for everyone involved.

This isn't to suggest that football with Hoeppner was a 9-to-5 proposition. Hep worked as hard, if not harder, than the next guy, but he found creative ways to include families whenever possible. On the weekends before the season started, Hoeppner wanted coaches to bring their families around practice whenever possible.

"In this business, it's easy to think that having your families around, or your kids around, is a distraction," said assistant coach Brian George, "and it's really just the opposite. Hep used it as a tool to teach our players and our coaches because he knew that we weren't going to treat our players badly if our sons and daughters were standing there on the sideline. But he also knew that our players were going to watch what they did as well."

And the families benefited greatly. It provided extra opportunities for the kids to see their dads. "I think it lessened the impact of our guys being away," Michelle Canada said. "It gave the kids a reason to love what their daddy does. And I can't tell you enough how great it was that Coach let us be around the players because they're such great role models to the kids. That was a privilege. It was invaluable the time he gave to the kids, the time he gave to my kids."

One rule Hoeppner had was that no weekly staff meeting would start before 8:15 a.m. That's because elementary school in Oxford, Ohio began at 8 a.m. Hep wanted to make sure his coaches were there in the morning when their kids woke up so they could help get them ready and then had the opportunity to drive them to school. "I can tell you this," said assistant coach Billy Lynch. "That doesn't happen in very many college football programs in America."

If someone had a family problem, whatever it might be, Hoeppner was always a great listener. In many ways, he would turn into a father figure instead of a boss. "He would always work with you when it came to your family," Brian George said. "If there was an issue, it was 'You need to take care of that first and we'll be fine.'"

Another thing Hoeppner did was invite the families of the coaches to dine with the team at the training table at least one night a week. On game day, all of the wives and families met at a designated area to greet their husbands and dads in a family-type environment.

"After the game, our wives and kids came down to the field to be with us, because it was important to both Hep and Jane," said Matt Canada. "The kids were going to be in the "Walk to the Rock." The bottom line was we are all in this together, and our families are going to be with us every step of the way. Hep and Jane made sure of it."

Miami athletic director Brad Bates said Hoeppner ran his football program with the same approach as his personal life. He wanted everyone to be family. "Jane was a surrogate mother in the same way that Terry was a surrogate father to those students who played for him at both Miami and Indiana," Bates said. "And the children and grandchildren were simply an extension of that family. It was a very large family and that's the way he wanted it.

"I think back often to his memorial service in Bloomington, and I was really taken aback. You could look around and see thousands of lives that Terry touched and inspired, and clearly the symbol of it all was his relationship with Jane."

✯ ✯ ✯

Bobby Johnson knew that Hoeppner was larger than life with his family. He was bigger than Santa Claus with his children. Johnson remembered one particular story with his daughter that the two men continued to laugh about for years to come.

One day at practice, Hep mentioned to Johnson that he thought his assistant coach looked tired. Johnson related a story from the night before regarding his four-year-old daughter Madilyn, who was having trouble sleeping. She had asked Daddy to lie down with her. Bobby told her he wasn't going to do that, and she went to her room crying. She told him she wanted him to be in trouble for not lying down with her.

"She didn't know who to talk to because I'm the dad and I'm the boss," Johnson said. "But she was smart enough to understand that when she came to practice, I listened to Hep, and that she had to listen to me, so maybe if she just went right around me and straight to Hep she'd be able to stay up later or Hep would make me lie down with her."

Johnson told Hoeppner the next day what happened, and he laughed and laughed. That night was Hoeppner's radio show, and Johnson and his family were in attendance. At a break in the show, Hoeppner walked over to Madilyn and said, "I heard you didn't want to go to sleep last night," and she told him that no, she had wanted her daddy to lie down with her, but that he told her she needed to lie down by herself like a big girl. And Hep looked her square in the eye and said, "Well you know what? The next time your daddy doesn't listen to you, you just call me."

Later that night, it was after 11 p.m. and Madilyn wouldn't lie down. She called Hep. A few minutes later she walked into the living room and handed her daddy the phone, and all Bobby could hear was Hep laughing hysterically on the other end.

"He was larger than life with my kids, and I think that was because he made himself so approachable with our family," Johnson said. "Hep gave me everything I could have ever wanted. All you want is to be treated like a man, shown some respect and your family to be treated properly. And those were things he always did."

Chapter 6
James Hardy

James Hardy never intended to play football at Indiana University. He was a basketball player first, and football was little more than an afterthought. In fact, he only started playing football his junior year in high school because the coach was short on bodies. He played, but the experts all agreed that Hardy's future in athletics was basketball.

He was an Indiana All-Star in high school and third in the balloting for the state's coveted *Indianapolis Star* Indiana Mr. Basketball honor, an award he believed he should have won. He liked IU coach Mike Davis and wanted to stay in state and play basketball at IU, but Davis wasn't the only one at IU that was interested. The football staff saw great potential for a big kid who could catch the football. Curt Mallory, son of former Indiana football coach Bill Mallory, was the lead recruiter on Hardy and urged then-IU coach Gerry DiNardo to make a scholarship offer. It couldn't have been a better situation for IU basketball. When the football offer was extended, IU hoop fans snickered at the thought that the Hoosiers had pulled one over on the system and got an extra basketball recruit who was coming to school on a football scholarship. Conventional wisdom was that the 6-foot-7 Hardy would play a year or two of football, but eventually would devote all of his time to basketball and count toward Davis' basketball scholarship allotment his final two or three years of college.

His first year at IU, nothing happened to change the perception. Hardy redshirted his freshman year in football in 2004, but played basketball and even made a couple of starts for Davis' squad. He played twenty-three games for the Hoosiers as a freshman. After the football season, though, DiNardo was fired, and Hardy was at a crossroads. He still wanted to explore football, but he didn't know about playing for a staff that hadn't recruited him. As for basketball, his relationship with Davis had deteriorated toward the end of his freshman basketball season. Davis wanted him to concentrate all of his efforts on basketball, while Hardy wasn't ready to give up the pigskin without playing at least one season. After DiNardo was fired, and with the uncertainty of who the Hoosiers would hire as their next football coach, Hardy actually considered quitting both sports and dropping out of school entirely. He was close to giving it all up and returning to his hometown of Fort Wayne, Ind. to begin life after athletics.

Looking back now, he's glad he waited around to see who IU would hire as its next football coach. Had he given in to the temptation to walk away after his freshman year, he knows now that he would have missed out on the chance of a lifetime, to say nothing of the friendship of a lifetime.

"I've always been one who has prayed about everything I do, and I always thought that the reason I was supposed to come to Indiana was to play basketball for Mike Davis," Hardy said. "I thought he was going to be the father figure that I had missed out on growing up. But after I met coach Hep, and I realized the type of person he was, I knew the reason I was supposed to come here was to meet him. My father figure wasn't supposed to be Mike Davis, it was supposed to be Terry Hoeppner."

Hardy remembers vividly the first one-on-one meeting he had with Hoeppner. Hep went on and on talking about his plan for IU, but Hardy wanted to interrupt and question how any of it had anything to do with a tall, skinny wide receiver like himself. As Hep talked, though, he started mentioning the spread offense he wanted to employ and the things he had been able to accomplish with Ben Roethlisberger at Miami of Ohio. Then he laid out his vision for IU football and included Hardy in his plan.

"He had never seen me play, and yet he looked at me and said, 'You've definitely got size, and from what I hear you've got good speed, too,'" Hardy recalled. "He thought we could work on some things and that I had a chance to be pretty good. He saw things in me as a football player that I really didn't see in myself. He believed in me as a person first, and as a football player second.

"And the reality is no one had ever really believed in me before. As I look back on it now, I just can't believe the vision that Hep had for me when you take into account that he was saying all of those things sight unseen. He looked at my physical attributes and saw potential, but when he talked with me, he told me later that he saw more than physical ability. He said he knew the kind of person I was from the first time we talked. I think it's fair to say that I felt the same way about him after our first conversation, too."

★ ★ ★

When you consider Hardy's upbringing, it's surprising in some ways that he and Hoeppner ever got together in the first place. Hardy's childhood was not one that generally has a happy ending.

When Hardy was five, his father, James Hardy Jr., was sent to prison for ten years for dealing drugs. For a decade, James Hardy III had no father figure. No role model. He wasn't taught a lot of things heading into college that he needed to know. He was street smart but lacked a lot of life's basics that a son acquires from his father.

He doesn't blame his father, and he does have a relationship with him today. What he learned from the experience was how much of an impact one bad decision can have on a person's life and the life of his family.

"I guess I could fault him for it because he could have gone the other way, but he was just trying to take care of his kids," Hardy said. "Coming from the type of environment that we came from, it was either this or that. He just chose the wrong side. He had a bad day, and it ended up costing him ten years of his life. I didn't see him from the time I was five until just after my freshman year in high school."

Without a father in the picture, and a rough life awaiting him at home every day, Hardy turned to sports as an outlet. He needed sports in order to gain the love and appreciation he wasn't experiencing at home. It wasn't that his family didn't love him; it was simply that with seven children in the Hardy family – two brothers and four sisters — there wasn't enough attention to go around.

"I always said to myself that I didn't want to go home because of the type of life I had to go home to, so I would just stay and work on my sport, whatever it was, and try to get better," Hardy said. "I'd stay in the gym rather than go home. When I played on my stage, which was sports, I always received a lot of positive attention. I always thought the better I got, the more people would come to watch me. And I figured if people enjoyed watching me play, that eventually I'd have a chance to use sports to do something with my life. Sports were where I experienced love."

Hardy ended up feeling love at IU, too, but it was more the kind you feel from family. After knowing Hoeppner and his wife Jane for just a very short time, Hardy felt loved.

After that initial conversation with Hoeppner shortly after Hep was hired at IU, Hardy and his new coach started meeting on a regular basis. That continued through spring football, into the summer of 2005 and eventually into Hardy's freshman season at IU. With Hoeppner making Hardy a focal point of the Indiana offense, Hardy put up big time numbers in his first season. He had 61 catches for 893 yards and 10 touchdowns. He was a freshman All-American by Rivals.com.

And he was starting to see in himself the things that Hoeppner had seen in him all along. Throughout that time, he and Hoeppner continued to get closer. "Each time I went to his office, it seemed like his wife would stop by and we'd just talk and laugh and enjoy each other's company," Hardy said. "And when I left he'd shake my hand, bring me to him for a hug, and tell me that he loved me. And I knew it was sincere. And I'd tell him I loved him, too."

✩ ✩ ✩

That love was put to the test in May of 2006 when Hardy was arrested for alleged domestic abuse of his girlfriend. Hardy pleaded not guilty, and his lawyers argued that the charges weren't true. He spent seventy-two hours in jail, however, in Fort Wayne and eventually posted a $1,500 bond. His girlfriend refused to prosecute and the charges were dropped.

For James Hardy, the three nights in jail were the lowest moments of his young life. Some of the things the policemen had said to him and accused him of at the time were extremely far-fetched, but he knew it would be his word against theirs and he worried aloud that there would be no one in his corner. He wondered if he had just thrown away everything he had worked so hard for at IU.

When he got out of jail, the first phone call Hardy made was to Hoeppner. When Hep answered the phone, Hardy could barely get the word 'Coach' out of his mouth, when Hep interrupted him. "He said, 'James, don't worry about it. I know it didn't happen like that. I know how it is. You handle what you have to handle and then just get down here as soon as you can, and we'll talk about it then. But,' he added, 'Know this. I'll never turn my back on you. I love you,' and I said, 'I love you, too, Coach.' And then there was a click."

When Hardy got back to Bloomington, Hoeppner had arranged a meeting for Hardy with himself, IU athletic director Rick Greenspan and IU president Adam Herbert. After Hardy explained exactly what had happened, Greenspan looked at him and said, "We've got your back. We're not going to let anything happen to you."

As they walked out of the meeting, Hoeppner told Hardy that things like this were a test of his character, and it was how he responded from that day forward that would tell the world what kind of person he was. Privately, he expressed some disappointment to Hardy that the situation had happened, but again made it clear that he would never waiver in his support. The experience helped make Hardy the man he is today.

"I was at the lowest point of my life, and this man was there saying he would always stand beside me," Hardy said. "I knew right then that I would love that man for the rest of my life. That was all about loyalty and he showed it. When we went back out to practice, all the media were coming at me, and he was right there with me. Before and after practice, he would ask me if I was OK, and then tell me I just needed to stay positive. And he told me he wasn't going to let anything happen to me.

"He took me under his wing, even though he had known me for less than a year. But we had talked so often that I felt like I had known him all of my life. That's why I tell people I felt like Hep was a father figure to me."

☆ ☆ ☆

Later that year, after Hoeppner had his second brain surgery in September of 2006, he and Hardy shared a special moment one day in his office. Hardy had stopped by to talk, and he sat with Hep and Jane in the IU football office and had lunch. Their conversation turned to Hardy, and he told his coach that he was doing OK, and not to worry. Hep looked Hardy square in the eye and said, "Honestly, I worry more about you than I do about myself."

That statement took Hardy aback. How could this man, who had recently endured his second brain surgery in ten months, be more worried about him than himself? The only way he could explain it was that Hoeppner truly did care for him very deeply. "He said he cared about me like I was one of his own," Hardy said.

Hardy was wearing a white tank top-like shirt that day, and underneath it Hep could see that he had a large, fresh tattoo. He asked him about it, and Hardy pulled up his shirt and showed him the tattoo he had gotten just a month before on the day his grandmother died. The tattoo was from Psalm 23, the familiar verse "Yea, though I walk through the valley of the shadow of Death, I will fear no evil for thou art with me. Thy rod and thy staff they comfort me." The words took up a large part of his upper chest.

"They looked at my tattoo, then they looked at each other, and they looked back at me, and I was like, 'What are y'all looking at?'" Jane replied that after he came out of his second surgery, the first words out of Hep's mouth were from Psalm 23. We then recited the Psalm together, and Jane said, 'God is good, and God brings people together for a reason.' It was a very inspirational moment for all three of us. We talked and laughed and hugged, and then we just walked out."

Hardy has three tattoos and doesn't add new ones without a lot of thought and consideration. Generally he will consider a tattoo for two or three years before actually opting to have it done. But he's thinking about adding a fourth as a tribute to Hep. "I've thought about it. There's no doubt about that," Hardy said. "If I do it, it's going to say 'Loyalty' because that's what I think of when I think of Terry Hoeppner. He made it clear to me that he would always stand by me, and he believed in me when few others did. It's that kind of undying loyalty that he and I will share even now that he's gone."

☆ ☆ ☆

Hardy's sophomore season was much like his rookie campaign. He caught 51 passes for 722 yards and 10 more touchdowns. His first two season totals were 112 catches for 1,615 yards and 20 touchdowns. Those 20 TDs had come in a total of 20 games.

As much as he enjoyed the individual accolades, Hardy was focused on bigger things heading into his junior season in 2007 – "Playing 13." One of Terry Hoeppner's visions for Indiana football was the concept of playing 13 games. That's significant because Indiana's schedule only has 12 games on it. To play a 13th game would mean that IU would finally get the monkey off its back and go to a bowl game for the first time since 1993.

"That's what I care about more than anything else this season," Hardy said a month before the start of the 2007 season. "Coach Hep talked about playing 13 games, and that's what we need to do to properly honor him. We're going to wear a patch on our jersey in his honor and a decal on the back of our helmet, but none of that is going to matter if we don't find a way to play 13 games."

☆ ☆ ☆

Though he only knew Hep a short time, Hardy has a wealth of memories of the man he called "Coach." Of all those memories, one stands out. It was the one and only time that Hardy went out to Terry and Jane Hoeppner's home, sometime late in 2006. Hardy was moving into a new apartment and was in need of a clothes dryer. Hoeppner had an old one in his garage and told Hardy to give him $20 and he could have it.

So Hardy went to the house and talked with Hoeppner's kids and grandkids. After a while, Hep told him to follow him because he had something to show him. He proceeded to take Hardy downstairs to the basement where he had what amounted to a trophy room with wall-to-wall memorabilia. He led Hardy around a corner and showed him an entire wall that had been dedicated to his prize pupil, former Miami of Ohio and current Pittsburgh Steelers quarterback Ben Roethlisberger. On the wall, there was Roethlisberger's college jersey, one from the AFC championship game, and assorted other keepsakes from the quarterback.

Opposite page: James Hardy makes a move after a catch in 2006 game action.

Then Hep pointed to a blank wall and said to him, "Now what do you think that's for?" "He looked at me, and I'm looking around, and finally I said, 'I don't know coach,'" Hardy said. "And he said, 'All of that is your space. I'm saving that to put up everything of yours. You're going to do it. I know you are. I just want to let you know that I'm proud of you already, but I know you're going to make me even prouder, and I wanted to make sure I had this wall space reserved so I can go out and brag about you, too.'

"And I mean, when he told me something like that, that just took me to another level. I was like, 'Man, he believes in me that much?' That day, I felt so good leaving his house that I went and worked out because I knew I could never let him down. I thought to myself that everything I have has come from God, and that God made him see something in me. It made me realize that one of my blessings and the reason why He sent me here was to meet coach Hep.

"As long as I live, I'm going to tell everybody who will listen what a great man Coach Hep was, and let them know all the things he did to help me become a man."

Chapter 7
Just for Kicks

Terry Hoeppner once said at Indiana that while he coached the majority of his football team, he harassed his kickers. It was all part of the soft spot he had in his heart for his players at the punting and place kicker positions. He worked with them every day in practice, put them in pressure situations to build up their confidence, and used golf analogies to help them combat the mental aspect of kicking. Basically, he did everything he could to build them up.

Oh, and he debated global warming with them, too.

At Indiana, before every practice, the Hoosiers worked on special teams. Hoeppner stood behind punters Tyson Beattie and Mike Hines and talked to them about a variety of topics. One day, Beattie walked over to back-up place-kicker Kevin Trulock and just shook his head about Hep's latest rant. "Whenever we're punting, he imposes all of his ideas on us," Beattie told Trulock. "He fills our ears with all this crazy stuff. The latest one is that he doesn't believe in global warming."

The next day, Trulock couldn't resist pulling Hoeppner's chain. It was hot outside, and Trulock walked up to Hep and said, "Man, it's really hot outside. It must be that global warming." Hoeppner looked at him, cocked his head to the side, and said, "Do you believe that stuff?" Trulock told him he did. Hep thought it was a bunch of garbage and went into a long explanation of what he had read on the subject. Trulock countered with his own ammunition.

"As a bio major, we've gone through all these mechanisms of chemistry and biology, and I broke down why I believed in it," Trulock said. "So Hep started printing off articles for me to read that supported his views. And this wasn't a one-time deal. It started early in fall practice (of 2006) and extended through the last conversation we had in winter conditioning (in 2007). We debated it literally every day before practice. And there were crowds of players coming up to listen. He took an extreme stance, and I took the opposite. At the end of the day I don't think either of us believed what we were saying, but the fun was in the debate. We had a lot of conversations like that."

If it wasn't global warming, it was something else equally nonfootball related. One day Trulock and Hep debated whether a man had really landed on the moon. "If it was debatable or controversial, we got into it," Trulock said. "In that case, he thought we landed on the moon, and I did, too, but I said we didn't and tried to give him all of this biological evidence. He'd listen to me until I was finished, and then he'd tell me how I was wrong. I tried to do the same, but I don't think I ever convinced him that he was wrong."

In the two years Trulock knew Terry Hoeppner, they talked very little about football and a whole lot about life. They had meetings scheduled for ten minutes that would last forty-five minutes to an hour. "As everyone knows, Hep was a very articulate person, and so we were kind of on that same level together," Trulock said. "We were able to discuss everything from philosophy to religion to politics. There was nothing taboo. Our relationship was fruitful from the beginning."

Many players at both Miami of Ohio and Indiana have talked about how Hoeppner was a father figure in their lives. Trulock counts himself in that company. His father, Steve Trulock, died of cancer when Kevin was thirteen, between his seventh- and eighth-grade years. Kevin spoke to Coach Hoeppner about his father many times, and Hep was always there to listen.

"I thought of Coach Hep as my friend, but I also thought of him as a father, as clichéd as that sounds," Trulock said. "He was a father in every sense of the word. And having lost my father, he was someone I could lean on from the very beginning. I guess I just had the feeling that I could do that."

When Hep was diagnosed with brain cancer, Trulock and his coach became even closer. "He was suffering from the same sickness as my dad, and I was so close to my father, so in a sense Coach took over that role for me," Trulock said. "We had some great meetings where we would talk about football for two or three minutes and everything else for thirty minutes or more. We knew we had to talk about football, but it was almost as if it was a formality to get to more important topics. We talked about his proton therapy treatment and were able to converse on a higher level. Since my dad had undergone cancer treatments, we were able to talk about all of that stuff."

There are many aspects of his relationship with Hep for which Trulock will forever be thankful. The most important, however, was that Hoeppner became like a father to him at a time when he needed one most. "I lost my dad when I was thirteen, a time when a lot of boys do their maturing," Trulock said. "Hep re-instilled for me the love and kinship between a father and a son. He rejuvenated that relationship for me. I'll pass down the relationship with my biological dad to my kids some day, but also the relationship I had with Hep. If you come to me ten or twenty years from now, when I have kids, you'll see Hep in my kids."

✷ ✷ ✷

Hoeppner's appreciation for his kickers began at Miami of Ohio. When he became head coach, working with special teams, and the kickers in particular, was part of the head coach's responsibilities. Every day at practice Hep would stand behind punter Kent McCullough with a stopwatch to track his hang time. When McCullough turned around, Hep gave him a number.

The ritual was repeated at every practice and in every pre-game warm up. In 2000, Miami of Ohio played a non-conference game at Ohio State, and McCullough's mother took a picture of her son warming up. Sure enough, Hep was right there in the frame with his stopwatch. (That photo appears at the beginning of this chapter.)

At the football banquet that year, McCullough had the picture framed with the engraving, "Thanks for watching my back." "Coach Hep always had my back, both literally and figuratively," McCullough said.

At that same banquet, Hoeppner had a gift for McCullough, too – the stopwatch. "He said he couldn't imagine timing anyone else with that watch, and then he presented it to me," McCullough said. "When I gave him that picture, it was my way of telling him that he was more than just a coach to me, and that I really appreciated everything. By him reciprocating the feelings, I knew he was even more special."

✷ ✷ ✷

Indiana punter Tyson Beattie marveled at several aspects of Terry Hoeppner, but none greater than the simple fact that Hep understood the kicking game. Beattie, a senior in 2006 who started all four seasons for the Hoosiers, said it's rare to find a head coach who is so in-tune with the kickers.

"Coach Hep understood the mental aspect of it and the pressures that we felt," Beattie said. "One of the most important things about Coach Hep was that he could relate to you. I learned later that Hep punted a little bit in high school, so maybe that's why he understood it all. It was good to be able to go in and say 'I didn't do well' or 'I choked' or 'I was nervous' and he actually understood. A lot of coaches don't."

Beattie found it entertaining the way Hoeppner used analogies between kicking and golf. His point was that you can perform any skill over and over, but when the moment comes where you have to nail it, sometimes you do and sometimes you don't. The key is repetition, and if you practice anything enough you'll improve your chances of success.

"He had other ways that he related to us as well," Beattie said. "He was a very intelligent guy. He read a lot, and he understood a lot of the sports psychology and the mental aspects of the game. He was a very deep thinker, and he helped us a lot that way."

★ ★ ★

Austin Starr's coming out party as a collegiate kicker came during the first week of October 2006 in Champaign, Ill. Starr split the uprights on a 33-yard field goal with no time remaining to lift the Hoosiers to a come-from-behind 34-32 victory over Illinois.

The kick was big on several levels for Starr. Making a pressure kick to win a game was big enough, but knowing he had his coach's confidence on the game's final play was even more important. Earlier in the fourth quarter, Starr missed a field goal from the same 33-yard distance. Even though television replays seemed to suggest that Starr had made the first one, too, he still had to wage the mental battle of not allowing history to repeat itself.

Just before Starr lined up for the potential game-winner, Hoeppner looked at his then-sophomore kicker and said, "Knock 'er through, dude." With the adrenalin rushing through his body, Starr said later he didn't remember what Hep said. Later that night it all came back to him, but the important thing was that he focused and made the kick. "The Illinois game put me in a light where people could say 'He could be somebody.'" Starr said. "And I owe that all to Hep. It was his belief in me that allowed me to make that second kick."

Hep's reaction to the 33-yard miss earlier in the quarter made the second attempt a hundred times easier for Starr. "After I missed that one kick, he just gave me support," Starr said. "It wasn't like, 'I can't believe you missed that,' or anything like that. Instead, he looked at me and said, 'You missed it, but you'll make the next one.' He always gave you hope, and in that situation he gave me hope for a second chance."

After the game, the entire IU team waited for Starr in the locker room. Coach Hep stood front and center, looked at Starr and said, "You did it." Starr looked back at Hep, "That was for you coach."

Starr felt like that was the moment he was able to repay Hep for the belief he had shown in him. In training camp, Hep went with Starr over Trulock in the battle of the place kickers. He then put Starr in situations where he could be successful, and his young kicker responded by making 12-of-15 for the 2006 season, with a long of 46 yards against Iowa.

Going into the 2007 season, Starr hoped to be able to repay his mentor for the last act he did before he died. Hep saw to it that Starr, a one-time walk-on, was given a scholarship to play football.

"At Hep's memorial service, his son Drew came up and told me, 'You know, he thought the world of you,'" Starr said. "For Drew to tell me that meant a lot. And because of that, everything I do (in the 2007 season) I'll dedicate to coach Hep and his family because they are the image of courage, strength and positive thinking."

Whenever Starr thinks of Hoeppner, he thinks of his coach's smile. At the memorial service, there was a brochure passed out with a picture of Hep's smiling face. Starr has the picture hanging up on the inside of his locker.

"I look at that picture right before I go out to practice, and it helps me focus on getting better," Starr said. "Hep's line was that you either improve or deteriorate. Looking at that picture, the words run through my mind, and I think to myself that at this practice anyway, I will improve."

✯ ✯ ✯

Even after Hep's passing, Jane Hoeppner has tried to keep the special bond between the kickers and the Hoeppner family alive. In early August of 2007, a month before Indiana's season opener, Jane had five kickers and special team members out to the family's home for dinner. There they interacted with grandkids and enjoyed some time reminiscing about Hep. "Jane is an amazing woman, and it's easy to see why they were such a wonderful pair," Beattie said. "Hep may be gone, but his memory lives in his family. Seeing them as often as we do really helps the healing process for all of us."

Chapter 8
Ben Roethlisberger

As a high school senior in Findlay, Ohio, Ben Roethlisberger lined up three schools to visit where he would potentially play college football. His first stop would be Durham, N.C. and the campus of Duke. The following week he would check out Miami of Ohio in Oxford, and his final visit was to be Ohio State.

After visiting Duke, Roethlisberger put the Blue Devils high on his list. He loved the campus and could really see himself going there. The next weekend, he and his parents made the trip to Oxford. Not surprisingly, Terry Hoeppner made quite an impression on that visit. At one point, as they were sitting in Hep's old office in Millett Hall, Hoeppner had to step out for a moment. Roethlisberger looked at his parents and said, "I want to commit to Miami right now. I want to say this is it." His parents talked him out of it, asking him not to make any snap decisions. They wanted him to go home, talk it over, pray, and make a decision from there.

"Well, we went home and within a day or so I cancelled my Ohio State visit," Roethlisberger said. "I knew that Miami was the place for me."

Roethlisberger first told people the reason he chose Miami was the chance to get a good education and play four years – and those things were important. "But in all truthfulness, ninety-five percent of the reason I went to Miami was to play for Terry Hoeppner," Roethlisberger said. "This was a guy with unbelievable enthusiasm and charisma, who believed in me."

∗ ∗ ∗

Shane Montgomery, who took over for Terry Hoeppner at Miami when Hep took the Indiana job in 2004, remembers fondly one of the first things that Hoeppner told him when he was interviewing for a position on Hep's Miami staff in 2001. Being from Ohio, Montgomery kept up with the Miami program, but he didn't really know the personnel. He did a little reading the night before the interview, but that was about it. During the interview they talked about how good Hoeppner thought the offense could be next season.

"I can still remember him saying, 'We've got this freshman quarterback that if you come in and don't screw him up, could be pretty good one day,'" Montgomery said. "And obviously we didn't screw Ben Roethlisberger up too much, but the words were vintage Hep."

∗ ∗ ∗

Terry Hoeppner loved to tell stories. He had a million of them, and many involved Ben Roethlisberger. Long after Hep left Miami, he would brag about his former quarterback. He loved to bring up the Kent State game in Ben's final season at Miami.

As Roethlisberger was thinking back on his favorite Hep stories, that same Kent State game came quickly to mind. In a magical 13-1 season that year for Miami, that game was one of the true gut checks. As Roethlisberger tells it, the RedHawks weren't playing well. It was midway through the fourth quarter and they were down by two scores. Hoeppner was really upset. He had just told some guys on offense to go down and tell Ben to pick it up and get going.

"But before they said anything to me, I walked up to Coach, and I said, 'Watch this.'" I went out, moved the team down field and threw a touchdown pass. After we got the ball back I went down and did it again, and we won the game. Hep said when I told him to 'watch this' he sat back and smiled. He thought I had grown up, and the fun was just beginning.

"I'm sure many coaches would be skeptical of their quarterback in that situation. But Coach Hep wasn't that way. He believed in me. He must have told that story a thousand times, in front of me many of those times. He told me later that when I walked up to him and said that during the Kent State game he was smiling on the inside and couldn't wait to see what was about to happen."

☆ ☆ ☆

One thing Roethlisberger knew about Coach Hep was he always had his quarterback's best interest in mind. Never was that any more apparent than a week or so before Roethlisberger and his Miami teammates faced Louisville in the GMAC Bowl at the end of his junior season.

Roethlisberger had been giving thought to declaring for the NFL draft and foregoing his final year of eligibility. Along with his parents, Roethlisberger went to the Hoeppner's home in Oxford one night to clear the air and talk about the possibilities. "We all sat down in their living room and talked about the pros and the cons, what I should and shouldn't do," Roethlisberger said.

What Roethlisberger found out very quickly was that his college coach had no intention of standing in his way. In fact, Hoeppner made his feelings perfectly clear during that discussion. "So many coaches in that situation would be selfish and know that if I stayed, it would help the program," Roethlisberger said. "But for Coach Hep, it was all about what was best for me. That's something else that made him so special. From the first time I told him that I was thinking about going, he was like, 'You know what? I think you're right. I think you're making the right decision.'"

When Roethlisberger heard those words he felt like a weight had been lifted from his shoulders. It certainly wasn't a conversation he was looking forward to having because of his loyalty to the man. But very quickly Hoeppner showed his true colors. "He sure made it easier on me. There's no question about that," Roethlisberger said.

★ ★ ★

Roethlisberger fondly recalls the day of the 2004 NFL draft at Madison Square Garden. Ben was the eleventh player selected overall in the first round by the Pittsburgh Steelers, and the third quarterback behind Eli Manning and Philip Rivers. Manning went first overall to San Diego, and Rivers was selected fourth. Eventually the two would be swapped in a trade.

With the New York Giants having the fourth pick overall, Terry Hoeppner was convinced that his college player was about to be taken off the board. He was eagerly anticipating Ben's name being called by the commissioner. "He swore up and down that he had talked to someone in the Giants organization and that I was definitely going there," Roethlisberger said. "And when the Giants didn't pick me, Hep threw his phone across the table, knocking a water bottle over in the process. He slammed back in his chair. All of these people were asking me who had thrown the phone. Was it my dad or my agent? I said, 'Nope, that would be my coach.'

"My attitude was whatever happened, happened. I was just thankful to be there, and I knew it was going to work out. But Hep was furious that I hadn't been the Giants' number four pick, because he had an inside scoop."

A little while later, Ben was picked by the Steelers and Hep was all smiles again. He was like a proud papa. "I remember how happy he was for me and how happy I was that he was there to share that moment with me," Roethlisberger said. "When my name was called, I remember giving my dad, mom and sister hugs. The next hug was reserved for him."

★ ★ ★

In three seasons at Miami, Roethlisberger had a 27-11 record. Off the field, however, he had a dismal 1-5-1 record in a sport that was dear to Hoeppner's heart. That was Ben's record when going one-on-one against Coach Hep on the golf course.

For the longest time, he was winless. But the last time they played together, when Ben was already with the Steelers, Roethlisberger found a way to beat his coach. "What I remember most about that was him making such a big deal about it. 'Oh, you finally got me. You finally got me,' he said. 'It's too bad we're not at Miami anymore so we could put it up on the JumboTron.'"

What Roethlisberger remembers most about golfing with Hoeppner were the close games and the conversations. "We would talk about so much," Roethlisberger said. "For a while we'd almost forget who was winning and who was losing. It was times like those that really allowed us to get closer."

It was through Hoeppner that Roethlisberger once got to play a round with Arnold Palmer. It was the Pennsylvania guys (Roethlisberger and Palmer) against the Ohio guys (Hoeppner and Spider Miller). "That was a blast," Ben said. "It was unbelievable getting to play with Arnold Palmer, and it was made more fun by the fact the Pennsylvania guys won. That was another time I technically beat him, but he wouldn't count it because I had Arnold Palmer on my team."

★ ★ ★

On the day of Roethlisberger's much publicized motorcycle accident in June of 2006, a mishap that would force the quarterback to undergo seven hours of surgery at Pittsburgh's Mercy Hospital, Terry Hoeppner was playing in a golf outing in Bloomington when he received the call.

Details were sketchy, but the caller told him that Roethlisberger had been seriously injured in a motorcycle accident. Hoeppner left his clubs in the golf cart and jogged toward the parking lot. He got in his car, drove home to pick up his wife Jane, and drove straight to Pittsburgh.

Outside of Cincinnati, they stopped at a rest area for a quick restroom break. They later said they really didn't want to stop, but nature called. It turned out to be fate. As Hep was walking back out to his car, he ran into Ken Roethlisberger and his daughter Carlee. Ken had been in

Cincinnati watching his daughter play in an AAU basketball tournament, while his wife Brenda stayed home. She was planning to go to Pittsburgh the next day anyway to film a Campbell's Soup commercial with her son. Like the Hoeppners, Ken and Carlee were headed to Pittsburgh as well. They wound up following each other the final 280 miles to be by Ben's side.

When they arrived at the hospital, Ben was in surgery. His mom had made the four-hour drive and was already there. The two families found out that Roethlisberger had suffered a broken jaw, had broken his left sinus cavity, suffered a nine-inch laceration to the back of his head, lost several teeth and had injuries where his knees hit the pavement.

As Ken Roethlisberger, his daughter and the Hoeppners tried to get into the trauma area to see Ben, a nurse stopped them at the door, saying only family was allowed in. Ken Roethlisberger looked the nurse in the eye, pointed to the Hoeppners, and said, "They're family."

"I remember knowing that Hep was there, although I was pretty much out of it," Roethlisberger recalled. "But you know, he always told me he would be there for me, and I shouldn't have been surprised that when I needed him, he was indeed."

That night in the hospital, Brenda Roethlisberger remembers looking down and seeing Hep still wearing his golf shoes from earlier in the day. Clearly, he was in a hurry.

✶ ✶ ✶

A few months later, Roethlisberger got to spend some quality time with his college coach again. In September of 2006, Hoeppner underwent his second brain surgery at Bloomington Hospital. Eighteen days later he was back on the sideline coaching his Indiana football team in the Big Ten opener against Wisconsin.

Coincidentally, the Steelers had a bye week in their schedule, and Roethlisberger was able to fly into Bloomington on Friday night. He got to spend some quality time with Hep and his family. "It was just an awesome experience," Roethlisberger said. "There was no place I wanted to be more that weekend than at that game with him."

The game was secondary compared to Hoeppner finding a way to make it back so quickly. For Ben, it was the second time he had seen this kind of Hoeppner performance. A month after his first brain surgery, Hoeppner had been Ben's guest when he played in the Super Bowl. In the Big Ten opener, "He was so excited to have me there and to be back coaching again," Ben said. "That was his love. After his family, his favorite thing was coaching. What I take away from that weekend is how excited he was. It was really good to see."

✫ ✫ ✫

Roethlisberger remembers a couple of phone conversations he had with Coach Hep the last few months of his life. "He was always trying to keep my head up because I was coming off a not-so-great season," Roethlisberger said. "A lot of the times we talked, he wouldn't tell me how bad it was. He didn't want me to worry. But I'd hear the truth from Drew (Hoeppner), so I had a pretty good idea."

A few days before Coach Hep died, Roethlisberger got a phone call from Drew Hoeppner, telling him that the doctors were making it clear things weren't looking good. Ben was in Los Angeles at a birthday party for his girlfriend, and he immediately got on a private plane for Indiana. He was in Bloomington the next day and was able to spend the weekend seeing Coach Hep and comforting the family. Terry Hoeppner died that following Tuesday morning.

"When I looked down at my phone that morning, I saw I had three missed calls from Drew, and right then I knew what had happened. So I called Drew and he told me. And I remember I didn't cry. I didn't cry all the way until the funeral. I think that was for a couple of reasons. One , when I had seen him a couple of days earlier I couldn't stop crying. But I think the big reason I didn't cry that day was that when

I had seen him earlier he didn't look like Coach Hep. I knew right then that he was in a better place, which was really reassuring. To know he wasn't hurting any more really did my heart good."

★ ★ ★

Terry Hoeppner's memorial service was held, fittingly, on the Saturday after he died because, as Jane Hoeppner put it, "It's Game Day." Once again, Roethlisberger chartered a jet, gathered eight of his buddies who had played for Coach Hep at one time or another, and headed to Bloomington. He wasn't looking for any fanfare though. He met his parents and his sister in Bloomington, and they drove over to the service together. He got there just a few minutes before the service started and then left before the IU players formed the tunnel for Coach Hep's hearse and funeral procession.

Roethlisberger admitted that he almost didn't even attend the service for the simple reason that he did not want to take away from Hep's day. "I didn't want the media to say, 'Oh, look who's here' and all of that. I didn't want that day to be about me at all. But the more I thought about it, I knew I had to be there. Not for Coach Hep, but for Jane and the family. I called Jane and said, 'If you want me there, I'll be there in a heartbeat,' and she said, 'Yes. I want you here and Coach would want you here, too.' And I said, 'OK, I'm there. There were no questions asked.' After it was over, I needed to get out of there. I saw the family before and after and I was good with that."

★ ★ ★

Roethlisberger collects jerseys from other professional athletes. Many of them are football players, but some are from other sports, too. He has their jersey framed and then puts two pictures underneath showing the athlete wearing it. He has jerseys from Joe Montana, Jerry Rice, Dan Marino and Jim Kelly to name a few, as well as basketball players Michael Jordan and Steve Nash.

He's about to add another jersey to his collection. It will be a college jersey of Terry Hoeppner from his playing days at Franklin College. Under the jersey, he's going to have a couple of pictures of Hep from his college days. "I'm going to put it on the wall in my game room, right between two of my prized possessions, my Michael Jordan jersey and my Derek Jeter jersey," Roethlisberger said.

It's fitting that Roethlisberger will have Hoeppner's jersey on his wall because his coach had two of Ben's jerseys framed in his basement. Ben got to see them when he was at Hoeppner's house the weekend of the IU-Wisconsin game in 2006.

"Seeing that at his house really meant a lot to me," Roethlisberger said. "It made me realize even more that this was a guy who would always have my back. I knew if I was ever in a fistfight, Hep would be right there ready to join the brawl. Some people are never lucky enough to meet a person like that. I'm very fortunate because I can always say that Hep was that guy for me."

Chapter 9
Don Fischer

Don Fischer, the voice of Indiana University football and basketball since 1973, will never forget the day he spent at the annual "Mad Anthony" Golf Tournament in Fort Wayne, Ind. in the summer of 2002.

Fischer got into a shuttle to go from the golf course back to the hotel after a practice round, and there was a guy sitting next to him who introduced himself, and quickly said "You're Don Fischer, right?" Well, the way Fischer tells the story, there were a lot of people on the shuttle talking, and he didn't catch the guy's name. And he didn't want to say 'What's your name again?' so he answered politely that he was indeed Don Fischer, and a smile enveloped the stranger's face. "I've listened to you for years," he said and then proceeded to ask one question after another about Indiana basketball. In a twenty-minute shuttle ride back to the hotel, Fischer estimated that the guy asked him fifty questions about things he had done, situations he'd been through, people that he knew. The guy was really engaging, and Fischer was wondering who he was. The only hint he had was the guy's ball cap with an "M" imprinted on the front.

"Do you know Steve Alford?" came the next question, and Fischer smiled and said that he knew Alford pretty well. "Oh, I know you do, Fish," the guy said. "I know Steve pretty well myself. He does his basketball camp in Franklin, Indiana, and that's where I started my coaching career."

That's when it clicked for Fischer. The "M" stood for Miami of Ohio, and Franklin College was the guy's first job. He was speaking to Terry Hoeppner. He knew from that first meeting that Hep was a hell of a guy.

The next year, Fischer was back at the same tournament and got paired in the practice round with former IU basketball player John Laskowski, former New York Yankee Johnny Blanchard, and Terry Hoeppner. And once again, Hoeppner spent the entire afternoon peppering Fischer with questions about IU. He never mentioned Miami of Ohio. He only wanted Fischer's insights on Indiana basketball and football.

At the end of the day, Fischer got on his cell phone and told his wife about the day and the fascinating conversation he had with Hep. "I told her that she wouldn't believe the guy I just played golf with that day. His name is Terry Hoeppner, he's the coach at Miami of Ohio, he's from Indiana, and you'd think he was the head coach at Indiana by what he knows about IU. And as I talked to her, I was thinking what a great fit he would be at Indiana University."

Fast forward a year. On Dec. 16, 2004, the day before Hoeppner was hired as coach, word got out that Hep was Indiana's man. When the news reached Fischer, he remembered telling the guy on the other end of the phone, "You've got be kidding me? We're getting the best guy we could possibly get!" From that day forward, he echoed those thoughts to anyone who would listen. "There was never a better fit for Indiana than Terry Hoeppner."

☆ ☆ ☆

The day Terry Hoeppner was introduced as the Indiana football coach he endeared himself even more to Fischer. Just a few minutes after IU athletic director Rick Greenspan introduced him, Hoeppner said one of the first things his grown kids had asked him after he accepted the job was if it meant they could meet Don Fischer. As a young coach in Indiana, and even later in his years at Miami, there were lots of chances to drive around the state on recruiting trips and the like. A staple for Hoeppner's family was finding a way to get Indiana football and basketball games on the radio and listen to Fischer.

"He was like part of our family," Hoeppner once said about the voice of IU athletics. "We'd be driving somewhere out in the middle of the nowhere and trying to get a station to come in, and all of a sudden we'd hear Fish's voice. It always made us feel like we were home."

From the first press conference, everyone Fischer talked to about Hoeppner said the same thing. They were all excited to have a head football coach who obviously wanted to be at Indiana more than any other place.

"Somebody asked him in the press conference about how difficult it was to tell his players at Miami that he was leaving, and Hep said it was one of the most difficult things he had ever had to do," Fischer said. "But he said if there was one job he would leave Miami for it was Indiana. That told you everything you needed to know about Terry Hoeppner. Right then a lot of people started rooting for him."

☆ ☆ ☆

Don Fischer started broadcasting Indiana football in the 1973 season. Lee Corso had taken over for John Pont as the IU coach that season, and Ken Starling was the captain. He would work with Corso for ten seasons, Sam Wyche for one, Bill Mallory for thirteen seasons, Cam Cameron for five, Gerry DiNardo for three and Hoeppner for two.

Fischer once told Hoeppner that he thought Hep was a combination of Corso and Mallory, an analogy he didn't think Hoeppner particularly liked. "I don't think he liked it because of Lee Corso's coaching ability, but what I meant was that I thought he brought the charisma, the energy and the personality of Corso, with the coaching ability, determination and toughness of Bill Mallory," Fischer said. "He combined characteristics of those two coaches into the best possible coach. And if you think about it, he was also a little bit like the Pied Piper. He got people to buy in right away."

Fischer pointed to Corso's history at IU as the perfect example. Corso was at Indiana for ten seasons, and left with a record of 41-68-2. His Big Ten record was 28-52-2. He had a total of two winning seasons and one of those was 6-5.

"How did he survive ten years?" Fischer asked. "Well, he did it with his engaging personality. He could get people to buy in to what he was trying to do. He had the support of the department and the university administration. Hep did exactly the same thing as Corso when he got here. He got the department and the administration on his side immediately. Then he went out and proved that he could coach."

From the start under Hoeppner, you could see that IU had a different football team than Hoosier fans had been used to. Hep wasn't afraid to take chances. "He basically went along with what everybody was thinking at the time, which was, 'Why would you be conservative at Indiana?'" Fischer said. "Why wouldn't you take chances? Why wouldn't you do things to at least give yourself a chance if being conservative wasn't getting it done?

"This is Indiana. We hadn't won. We needed a coach willing to take chances, and that's what he did. And people loved that because they were all thinking the same thing, namely, 'What do you have to lose?' He engaged people with his personality and hooked them with the way he coached."

The other thing Indiana wasn't used to was a coach trying to start some traditions. Hep went and got "The Rock," and he started "The Walk." While those might not seem like big deals, they were to a program struggling for an identity. "He tried to get things started so people understood that this is a place to be proud of," Fischer said. "Even though we haven't had tremendous football success over the years, we could do better. Starting tradition is part of that success."

Fischer has heard his share of people outside of Indiana make disparaging remarks about "The Rock." Some have called it "The Pebble," and others think it was just one more gimmick from a guy they referred to as "Coach Hype." "You know what?" Fischer said. "Those players don't make jokes about it. They loved that thing. And they loved the idea of "The Walk." Those kinds of things were never here before. Hep brought pizzazz along with great coaching ability and a winning personality."

★ ★ ★

Hep and Fischer both loved to play golf. Fischer was lucky enough to accompany Hoeppner on his final eighteen holes on December 18, 2006. The night before, Terry and Jane Hoeppner were over at Fischer's home in Greenwood for a party with those who worked on the football radio broadcast. It was unseasonably warm for December and Fischer mentioned to Hep that he was going to play golf the next day. Hep's eyes lit up, and he asked Fish if he needed someone to play with him. When Fischer said he did, the pair decided to meet at Bloomington Country Club at noon the next day.

"What people may not know about Hep was that he was dealing with a bad hip a lot of the time he was at IU," Fischer said. "He probably should have had it repaired the year he got here, but he was too busy with all of his speaking engagements around the state to get it done that summer, and then he didn't want to be on the sidelines in crutches during the season. So he put if off. His hip struggles, coupled with the football season, had really limited his opportunity to play any golf since the summer."

They played eighteen holes that day, with Hoeppner struggling because of his hip. "He was mad," Fischer said. "He couldn't follow through because of his hip, and he couldn't go back as far on his backswing, so he started hitting balls all over the place. By the end of the afternoon, he was disconsolate. He wasn't hitting the ball as well as he liked to, and of course we had a two-dollar bet on each side, which he lost.

"But here's something about Hep. As mad as he was about the way he was playing, he never made me feel like he wasn't having fun. We were still having a good time, and he still made cracks about his swing and stuff. He was always fun to be around. He never made you feel like he didn't want to be there."

✻ ✻ ✻

There are a lot of things about Terry Hoeppner that Fischer always marveled about: his passion, his energy, his spirit and his all-out devotion to his wife Jane. It was obvious that other people felt the same way. Fischer never met anyone who had anything negative to say about Terry Hoeppner.

"Never. Not once," Fischer said. "I've never met anyone who had a negative word to say about Hep. And I talk to people every day. Ever since his first surgery, every single time I would see someone, they would always ask how Hep was doing. That tells you what kind of impact he had on the fan base at this university, and it gives you a little glimpse as to why people loved him the way they did. I think about him every day. I can't tell you how much I'm going to miss him."

Chapter 10
Anthony Thompson

The first time Anthony Thompson met Terry Hoeppner Hep offered him a job. It was Hoeppner's first day on the IU campus and when Rick Greenspan introduced him to the former Indiana All-American running back, there was a flash in the coach's eyes. The former IU great barely got out the words, "Coach, I'm Anthony Thompson," before Hep fired back, "Oh, I know who you are." What people didn't know about Hoeppner then was that he was well-versed in Indiana University lore. He knew the history of the football and basketball programs in particular. For the most part, he had lived them growing up in the state of Indiana. And any loyal Hoosier fan knew A.T. This was a guy who finished second in the Heisman Trophy balloting behind Houston's Andre Ware. After the two spoke for just a few minutes, Hoeppner asked Thompson if he'd like to be IU's running backs coach. Hep wanted the opportunity to work with him side by side.

While Thompson had to decline Hoeppner's coaching offer, little did the two know that before too long the side-by-side prophecy would be fulfilled. It wasn't a coach-to-coach relationship, though. Instead, the pair became close on a much different level. For the last eighteen months of Terry Hoeppner's life, Anthony Thompson was by his side as his pastor.

Thompson had actually done the coaching thing before at his alma mater. When Cam Cameron was hired prior to the 1997 season, he made Thompson his running backs coach.

When Cameron was fired after the 2001 season, Thompson pursued a different calling. While he continued to work at Indiana as a fundraising officer in the IU Varsity Club, Thompson founded his own church in Bloomington, the Lighthouse Community Church. Always a very spiritual man (as a player he always kept a Bible in his locker), Thompson finally was realizing his dream of doing the Lord's work.

✴ ✴ ✴

Thompson was close to two Indiana football coaches in more than twenty years at the university. There was Bill Mallory, the man whom he played for from 1986-89 at IU, and Terry Hoeppner, the man with whom he shared a special relationship in the last two years of Hep's life. There were obvious similarities between the two.

"The one thing about both Coach Mallory and Coach Hoeppner was they cared about people," Thompson said. "They both respected people. One of the things that drew me to Indiana was Coach Mallory. He was like a father to me. And Coach Hep was the same way with James Hardy and all the other kids. He believed in them when nobody else did. He could see something that other people couldn't. Something I'd say about both Coach Hep and Coach Mallory is that they believed in people, and they treated them the way they would want to be treated themselves."

One thing Thompson knew about both coaches was that they were the same person in private that they were in public. "Hep was always the same guy," Thompson said. "He didn't have to put on any false face. He wasn't pretentious in any way. What you saw was what you got. It was that way with Coach Hoeppner, and it was clearly that way with Coach Mallory, too."

Another similarity, as Thompson saw it, was that both Mallory and Hoeppner had a great passion for Indiana University. "With Coach Mallory, it was never about him," Thompson said. "He loved the university and the football program so much, and he knew it was about these kids and the people who helped build this program. And the same was true with Coach Hep. This was his dream job. He knew IU and the people that were here. He knew Anthony Thompson before Anthony Thompson knew who he was."

Most of all, what Bill Mallory and Terry Hoeppner shared was contagious enthusiasm. "Coach Mallory had it, and Coach Hep most definitely had it," Thompson said. "They got people to believe in their vision. And I think that's a gift. Whatever it was, they had it."

✯ ✯ ✯

When Thompson looks back on the time he spent ministering to Terry and Jane Hoeppner, he describes the experience as a journey and a whirlwind. Everything happened so fast. His first memories of Hoeppner from a ministry standpoint came after Hep initially got sick.

"When the illness came about, I think he experienced a newfound relationship with Christ," Thompson said. "I remember sitting there with him and Jane, and he said, 'After going through this, I know my purpose now. God has given me a second chance and I'm going to make the best of it.'"

Thompson recalled a time in the spring of 2006, following Hoeppner's two surgeries. The coach was weak after undergoing radiation. "I remember sitting there with him, and he had no strength," Thompson said. "He could hardly get up. He was kind of confined to a chair, and he looked at me with this puzzled look and said, 'What ways can I really exemplify or express my faith?' And I told him, 'Coach, don't worry about that. God will make a way.'"

Thompson and another minister, Pastor David Beacham of Apostolic Bible Church, went out to Hoeppner's house regularly to bring him communion and share the Word. It was in those visits that Thompson experienced a truly amazing Christian experience. While he went there to try to encourage Terry and Jane, they would end up encouraging him. "They flipped the script so to speak," said Thompson. "It was amazing. That's kind of where the journey began. We sang praise songs. He shared with me what scripture he and

Jane were reading that day and we'd have devotion together.

"He and Jane would get up every morning and recite scripture. They'd recite healing scriptures, and scriptures of comfort. Then I'd come in and talk about the sermon I preached on Sunday, or what Bible study I was leading. We had those kinds of experiences all the way up until he died."

★ ★ ★

One of Thompson's most vivid memories of Hoeppner came the night before Hep had his second brain surgery on September 13, 2006. The day before, Hoeppner told his team about the next day's surgery and then held a hastily called press conference that evening to tell the media Bill Lynch would be assuming the coaching responsibilities and to answer questions about the expected timetable for his return.

After Hoeppner spoke with the team that day, Jane asked Anthony Thompson and his wife Lori to step into Hep's office and pray with them. The prayer was what one would expect. They prayed that God would see Hep through the surgery, and that He would give him the strength he needed and would comfort the family.

The Sunday after Hoeppner had his second brain surgery, he showed up unannounced at Thompson's morning church service.

"We were welcoming our visitors, and I looked up, and Hep and Jane were walking down the aisle," Thompson said. "And he gave this little sermon. He didn't know anybody in the church except my wife and me, but he looked at me and said 'This is my chance.'"

And in typical Terry Hoeppner style he said, 'I want to tell you something.' And he started talking about the goodness of the Lord. He talked about the miracle, and how he was blessed and honored to be given a second chance. He wanted to thank the people for praying for him and lifting him up. It was very emotional and moving. His presence there that day really left a mark on all of us."

★ ★ ★

In Hoeppner's final months, there was speculation that the family was hiding Hep's condition from the public because they didn't want anyone to know how bad things were getting for the patriarch of the family. Make no mistake, the Hoeppner family wanted its privacy at that difficult time, but it wasn't because they had something to hide. They just wanted some time to allow him to focus 100% on the situation at hand. Everyone in the Hoeppner family shared the belief that cancer was a temporary obstacle, and one he was going to find a way to beat.

One of the things Thompson admired about Hoeppner until the very end was his resolve. A day didn't go by that Hoeppner didn't talk about getting better. "I don't think he ever believed that this illness would take his life," Thompson said. "I mean I'm sure there were times when he was down, because he was only human. But he never indicated that to anyone. He and Jane were very confident.

"The only reason I was able to come out of there speaking positively was Jane and Terry's belief. They had trust in the Lord and the Lord gave them the comfort to be able to say and do all those things. It wasn't like they were hiding anything; they just wanted their privacy. They didn't want people to cast doubt on the situation. They didn't want any negative thoughts. They were positive people, and they were convinced that he was going to be OK"

Looking back, Thompson said he realizes that he was one of the final people who ever had the privilege to hear Terry Hoeppner speak. They were conversations between a believer and his minister. "I'm telling you the words he spoke were ones of encouragement," Thompson said. "He never asked me to tell the team something because he didn't think he was going to make it. He believed he could overcome his illness right up until the end. Sometimes he just wanted to share scripture with me or talk about the Lord. It wasn't fake or a façade or anything like that. It was him and it was genuine."

★ ★ ★

Thompson learned countless life lessons from Terry and Jane Hoeppner. In the end, he learned how to live and he learned how to die. "I told the people at the Big Ten Kickoff Luncheon (in August of 2007) that Terry taught us how to live, how to suffer and how to die with dignity," Thompson said. "I've seen him not just live, but live life to its fullest. And I've seen him suffer with dignity. I've seen him hurting, and yet when he knew that you were worried about him, he would say, 'Hey, don't worry about me. I'll be OK' I saw him strong until the very end.

"I knew he was in pain, but when I was there he never complained. Even in his suffering he talked about his belief in God. The whole experience was just amazing. It's hard for me to even describe. This was just a remarkable man who lived his life the same way from beginning to end."

Thompson reiterated his point about the road his relationship with Hoeppner followed. "It was a journey," he said. "We didn't know how long the journey was going to last, but when I reflect on it, I can't help but think of the things I learned from him. And I'll tell you this. That's how I'd want to go out – with dignity and with my belief system intact. In his case, I believe he went out having enjoyed the ride."

✯ ✯ ✯

When Anthony Thompson looks back on the two-and-a-half years that Hoeppner spent at Indiana, he doesn't marvel as much at Hep's accomplishments. When he thinks about all of the speaking engagements and the ways that Hoeppner tried to build traditions and get people excited at IU, he knows it was all just part of the plan – God's plan.

"When I look back on it now, it was all in God's plan," Thompson said. "The process had to be speeded up because God knew how long he was going to stay here on this earth. I believe God gave him the favor of being able to go and speak and capture the hearts of so many people. People called him the Pied Piper, and that's what he was. It's just that his time was short, and we didn't know it."

Chapter 11
Indiana Players

When Terry Hoeppner arrived on the Indiana scene in December of 2004, the IU football program was at rock bottom. The 2004 season ended with a 63-24 thrashing in the Old Oaken Bucket game at Purdue, a loss that sealed the fate of former IU coach Gerry DiNardo. First-year athletic director Rick Greenspan always maintained that he'd judge the IU football program on a complete body of work, but moments after the Hoosiers lost to Purdue in West Lafayette, it was clear that Greenspan would be looking for someone new to direct the Indiana program.

Under DiNardo, morale was at an all-time low. And not just within the football program. Administrators tiptoed around DiNardo and his "my way or the highway" approach. More than one associate athletic director told of how he had been barred from attending football practice, and players talked in private about never feeling comfortable interacting with their head coach.

All of that changed almost overnight the day Indiana hired Terry Hoeppner as its new head football coach. The official announcement came on December 17, 2004. Greenspan got players not on Christmas break to meet with Hoeppner, and later, when everyone was back, held a more formal meeting where Hep met the entire team. Shortly after he was named IU's head coach, Hoeppner sent an e-mail out to everyone on the team briefly introducing himself and expressing his interest in meeting each of them individually.

A select group of players – those who would be seniors in the fall of 2005 – got more than just the e-mail. "I was out in Phoenix for Christmas break, and I get a phone call from this guy, and he says, 'This is Terry Hoeppner, and I'm your new football coach,'" said Russ Richardson, a senior on Hoeppner's first IU squad. "He said, 'We're getting ready to do this press conference, but I wanted to call all the seniors first and let you know I'm excited to have you on my team and I'm on fire to have this class. I don't really know you yet, but I can't wait to work with you guys.'

"It was a small gesture, and I didn't know the man, but it made a great first impression. He had a crazy day, all kinds of meetings and different things going on, but before he did his press conference he called every one of us seniors to let us know that he cared about us."

After Christmas break, Richardson and his teammates got to meet their new coach in person. From that very first meeting, IU players were convinced that things were going to be different with the Indiana football program. Hoeppner walked into the room that day full of life, energy and enthusiasm. It was the same way he would walk into every meeting from that day forward, and players found it a welcome relief.

"Right away, I knew he was an approachable guy," said long snapper Tim Bugg. "Previously we were around an intimidating coach who was not very approachable, but when I met coach Hep he was open, friendly and easy to talk to. I could tell right away that he was somebody I could go to if I ever needed anything."

Tackle Charlie Emerson recalled that first meeting seeing Hoeppner walk in the room with a huge smile, decked out from head to toe in IU gear. More than anything else, you could sense that Hoeppner was proud to be there. "I remember he talked about how Indiana was his dream job, and that this was all he ever wanted to do," Emerson said. "But you just knew from that first moment that this was going to work. He was super excited about wanting this program to succeed. From the get go, everyone felt his energy and excitement. Everyone loved him. He was 100% IU, and we hit the ground running."

Defensive lineman Greg Brown first met Hep on a recruiting visit to Miami of Ohio when he was in high school. He liked the coach but wanted to play in the Big Ten and chose Indiana. When the Hoosiers hired Hoeppner, Brown first learned about it on TV over Christmas break and then in Hep's e-mail to the team. When he and his teammates met Hoeppner after the break, Brown knew from the very first moment Hep walked into the room that changes were about to be made.

"You could feel the change immediately," Brown said. "The first thing he said to us was that we didn't have problems, we had opportunities. And I think a lot of people in the room sat up a little straighter and started to listen. The more he talked, the more excited you got. Very quickly people realized that this was the guy who was going to take us places we had never been before. I don't know how to describe it other than to say that you just knew it when he walked into the room. You had this feeling like, 'This dude is good.'"

Will Meyers was another one who'd been recruited by Hoeppner to Miami of Ohio. When word got out that Hoeppner was the new IU coach, Meyers said his initial reaction was shock – in a good way. "My first thought when he became our coach was 'Wow, I can't believe we got this guy,'" Meyers said. "I had followed Miami and Coach Hep since he recruited me, and I knew what caliber of coach he was, so when we got him I was ecstatic. I knew the energy and passion he brought to the table was exactly what this program needed."

Josiah Sears had a different first meeting with Hoeppner. The big fullback had put on a few pounds in the off season, and the coaching staff was considering moving him to the defensive side of the ball. Sears didn't want any part of it, so Hep made him a deal. He told him he either had to gain twenty pounds to play defense, or lose ten and stay on offense.

"So I went out and lost ten pounds in about four days. Hep thought that was the funniest thing he had ever seen," Sears said. "He found it pretty amusing that I was willing to lose weight so I didn't have to put my hand on the ground and play defense."

Not everyone initially bought into what Hep was selling. Defensive back Tracy Porter admitted he was a reluctant follower at first. "I was a young guy, and I really didn't buy into all of the new coach hype," Porter said. "I wasn't too fond of him when he first came in because I had a stubborn attitude. I was still that way a little bit in the spring, and at that point I think he knew I wasn't real happy so he called me into his office to talk about the things he believed in."

They also talked about Porter's role on the team and how Hoeppner believed he could be a major contributor. "Every coach is going to say that to you, so sometimes you think you're getting lip service," Porter said. "But it was different with Hep. The way he talked, you knew that he genuinely believed what he was telling you. Coming out of spring practice, I had a different attitude. He really turned me around, and I feel like he helped mold me into the man I am today."

✩ ✩ ✩

IU players have countless memories of the man they called Hep. But the one thing that stood out more than anything else was his infectious smile. Long snapper Tim Bugg called it "a big, jolly smile." Tackle Charlie Emerson added, "After one of his corny jokes, he'd just sit there and smile. Or he'd deliver one of his sayings, look at everybody and watch it sink in. He'd see the smiles come over everybody as they thought about what he just said. It was Hep's complete look of happiness that I know I'll never forget."

Andrew Means marveled at how it seemed like Hep never had a bad day. He was like a bright sun always shining down on his players. "If he was down, you never knew it. He always had his team up. He was vibrant and energetic. When I remember Hep, I'll remember this big, bright sun."

For Sears, Hep's image is the photo of him with arms raised above his head in a triumphant position. "He loved IU and that's what I'll always remember about him," Sears said. "He poured everything he had into this place. You knew he loved the state of Indiana and Indiana University, and he wanted the absolute best for us."

Will Meyers' image of Hep is a face with gritted teeth, and a man with unrivaled drive and determination. "I think of a guy who was not willing to accept the status quo," Meyers said. "That involved Indiana football, what people thought of us, and what we thought of ourselves. It included losing or even just being behind. He was never going to accept it."

Hep's confidence more than anything else was special to Tim Bugg. Hep told the team every day how good they were, and he never stopped building them up, even when adversity hit. It was important to the coach that his players knew how much he believed in them. "And we believed," Bugg said. "When Saturday rolled around, we were ready to play. We didn't win every game, in fact we lost more than we won, but after every game he always told us what we needed to hear. He let us know what we did wrong, but he also told us that we were a great team and still had a chance to do something special. He always believed we had a chance. His confidence was contagious."

★ ★ ★

IU's seniors from the 2005 season weren't sure what to expect from Hoeppner. The day he was hired was refreshing, but they weren't sure if that would mean anything by the time the season rolled around. While it was nice for a coach to think positively, the reality was that these guys were afraid they might get kicked to the curb so that Hep could build a foundation with younger players.

Nothing was further from the truth. Guys like Victor

Adeyanju, Adam Hines, Kyle Killion, Will Lumpkin, John Pannozzo, Isaac Sowells and Richardson, to name a few, were given the royal treatment by their new head coach. "My senior class was a bunch of 'not enough's,'" Richardson said. "We didn't have enough height. We didn't have enough weight. We were all the last guys to get picked in the recruiting class because DiNardo needed recruits fast. So they took a chance on a bunch of us.

"It would have been real easy for Coach Hep to come in and look at our size and just say, 'You know what, let's just scrap these cats and start thinking about the up-and-coming players.' But he and his staff embraced us and treated us like men. People talk a lot about a 'player's coach,' but the best kind of player's coach is one that a player would do anything for. And Hep was that guy to us."

✰ ✰ ✰

For Tracy Porter, the lesson learned was that there really is such a thing as the student-athlete in college athletics. Porter struggled academically his first year at IU and was on academic probation after a 1.9 grade point average his freshman year. When Hoeppner came on board, he made some changes regarding what he expected academically from his team. He incorporated some extra study tables and made it clear that he expected his players to excel not just on the field, but also in the classroom. Porter will forever be grateful for what Hep did for him not only as a football player, but as a student, too.

"The guys who were struggling academically were required to have so many hours at study table, and Hep monitored it very closely," Porter said. "My freshman year I came in unfocused, and not applying myself hurt my grades. But when Hep came in, he pushed me hard both on and off the field. After a while I realized, 'Hey, he's for real.' I bought into everything he was trying to teach me and was able to get things turned around."

Porter was clearly one of Hoeppner's academic success stories. In the last semester before Hep's death, forty-six Indiana football players made the honor roll, a point that was a great source of pride with the IU football coach. Perhaps making Hep even prouder was having Tracy Porter among those players. His G.P.A. ended up being 3.1.

Porter felt his academic performance was another example of Hoeppner's vow to never quit. "I feel like I've lived that 'Don't Quit' poem," he said. "My G.P.A. was terrible coming into my sophomore year. But he told me it wasn't the end of the world. He said I could still get things turned around. I believed that, and I started applying myself in school and didn't quit. I always felt that if he was willing to work that hard for me, I could certainly work that hard for him on the football field."

The other lesson Porter learned was that good things happen when you believe in someone. "It meant a lot to know that even though Hep didn't know me or recruit me, he took the time to come and talk to me and get me straightened out," Porter said. "Everybody was proud to have Hep as their coach."

☆ ☆ ☆

The on-the-field memories of Hep were bountiful as well. IU was 9-14 in two seasons under Hoeppner, but included in those nine victories were a couple of major wins for the program. In 2006, the Hoosiers knocked off No. 13 Iowa, 31-28. Two weeks later, IU beat Michigan State, 46-21, to get to five victories, within one game of being bowl eligible, with three to play.

With the Iowa game in particular, players knew when Hep walked in the locker room before the game that this was a game they would win. It was something about the fire in his eyes that day.

"He walked in and said flat out, 'We're going to win this game,'" said Greg Brown. "He was always confident, but something was different that day. I don't know what got into him, but it made you think, 'We can't let him down.'"

Another memorable game in 2006 was Illinois at Champaign, when Austin Starr got a second chance at a game-winning field goal and connected from 33 yards to give IU a 34-32 victory.

IU players talk about an incident that happened hours before kickoff to set the tone for the day. Indiana spent the night at what players described as a "run down motel" in Danville, Ill. The morning of the game they had a pre-game meeting before they boarded the buses. The hotel personnel set it up in a smoky bar on the property, with the assistant coaches sitting on bar stools and the players at tables.

"Coach Hep walked in and was furious about the conditions," said Charlie Emerson. "He started yelling about how disrespectful it was to set us up in this bar. He canceled the meeting and told everybody to get on the bus. His fire and tenacity really rubbed off on us. He was angry that morning, and it made us angry, too. We went out and had a great game that day."

Will Meyers remembers another story from that game. In the first quarter, the Illini used several trick plays and were able to do anything they wanted on offense. They scored twenty-two first quarter points, and the IU defense couldn't get out of its own way. Early in the second quarter, co-defensive coordinator Joe Palcic had the defense huddled on the sideline and was altering their schemes, when an angry Hoeppner came over and threw his headset on the ground. "He looked at us and said, 'Scrap it all,'" Meyers recalled. "We were going straight man-to-man. We'd blitz on every down and just lock on our man the rest of the game.

"I was kind of shocked. It was like something you'd do on the playground. I couldn't believe that was our plan. But it worked. We totally scrapped everything we were going to do, and we played that way the rest of the game. We blitzed our linebackers and it made for quite a memory."

But the memories weren't only made in the victories. In 2005, Hep's first year at IU, the Hoosiers went to Michigan, needing a victory to stay alive for a possible bowl game. IU was 4-5 going into the game, but the 41-14 loss to No. 21 Michigan that day in the Big House ended any Hoosier bowl hopes once and for all.

Three minutes into the game, though, things were looking good for Indiana. Blake Powers and Jahkeen Gilmore hooked up on a 42-yard touchdown pass on IU's first possession, and the Hoosiers led, 7-0. Michigan would go on to score 41 unanswered points, but with 11:57 to play in that first quarter the scoreboard read: IU 7, Michigan 0.

"We go in and score on that first possession, and I remember Hep turning around and looking at me, saying, 'It's quiet in the Big House, isn't it?'" said kicker Kevin Trulock. "And I said, 'Yeah, it sure is,' and he had this very satisfied look on his face."

★ ★ ★

Russ Richardson only played one season for Hoeppner, but as it turned out, he may have been one of the last players to spend some quality time with Hep before he died. In March of 2007, Richardson flew from Phoenix back to Indiana to talk to his former assistant coaches and Hep about some life-changing plans he was considering. Even though he had a good job in Phoenix as a marketing specialist for a large furniture company, Richardson was thinking about returning to IU in the fall to get his MBA at the Kelley School of Business in Bloomington.

When he arrived in town, Richardson called Hoeppner. He knew his coach was sick, but he wasn't sure how sick. He told Hep he wanted to talk with him about some life-changing plans. Hep asked if they could meet the next day in the IU football coaching offices.

The following day, Richardson first met with assistant coach Brian George. At some point in the conversation Richardson told him that Hep was coming over to meet him around noon. George was taken aback. "Coach Hep is coming here to talk to you?" he asked. "Yeah, I've got some im-

portant things to talk with him about," Richardson said. "Hep hasn't been around very much. He's come in a couple of times to talk with the coaches, but if he's making a special trip for you, that's some pretty cool stuff," George responded.

Hep arrived a little bit later, with Jane not far behind. She brought Taco Bell for the three to dine on – "Hep liked those Gordita Crunch Wraps," Richardson said. He then told Hep about his plan and asked his opinion. Hoeppner told him how his Masters had taken him about ten years to complete, one class per year as he coached, but how proud he was of the accomplishment. Richardson told his former coach that what worried him the most was the risk of giving up the job he had in Phoenix. At some point, Hep interrupted him and told him he was convinced Richardson was making the right decision, and that it was important not to be afraid to take risks.

"We wound up talking for two hours about a variety of topics. He told me how his health issues had brought him closer to the Lord and closer to his wife, and for those two things he could never be more grateful," Richardson said. "When I think that less than three months later he died, it blows me away. He was so sick, and yet all he worried about was what he could do for a 6'0", 255-pound Big Ten nose guard he only knew for a year. That tells you all you need to know about Terry Hoeppner."

During the conversation that day Richardson tried to find out about Hep's health, but his coach obviously didn't want to dwell on that. He gave a quick response and then changed the subject back to Richardson. His response was vintage Hep. "You know, I'm kind of like the title of that new Toby Keith song," Hoeppner told him. "I'm not as good as I once was, but I'm as good once as I ever was."

✯ ✯ ✯

Indiana quarterback Kellen Lewis' memory of Terry Hoeppner from early 2007 will always define his coach.

Opposite page: Coach Hoeppner roams the sidelines in a game at Memorial Stadium.

Hoeppner called Lewis, James Hardy and a few of the other veteran players into his office to talk about the upcoming 2007 season. In the past, he had always focused on Indiana's goal to "Play 13" (which meant a bowl game). But on this day he didn't want to talk about IU playing in just any bowl. He wanted to talk about *the* bowl.

As the players came in one by one, he handed each of them a single red rose and said it was never too early to dream. "He told us he had been to the Rose Bowl just a few weeks before, and he took the opportunity to scope everything out for us," Lewis said. "He was checking out the hotels and trying to figure out where we would be staying and all of that. Part of you always laughed when he did something like that, but in another sense it was what made him such a great coach. He had his plan and he was working it. That's why every guy on this team would run through a wall for the guy."

Chapter 12
Miami of Ohio Players

When the wife of former Miami of Ohio defensive standout Ron Carpenter died in May of 2005, Carpenter wasn't surprised to see a call coming in the day of the funeral from Terry Hoeppner, his former defensive backs coach. Carpenter was just leaving his house and heading for the service. Even though it had been thirteen years since Carpenter had played at Miami, he and Hoeppner had stayed in touch. When he saw the number, Carpenter thought it was nice that Hoeppner was calling to offer his condolences.

But that wasn't why Hep was calling. Instead, he was calling to tell Carpenter that he and his wife Jane were on their way and would be at the funeral in person. "It meant a lot to me, but I wasn't surprised because that was the type of guy Hep was," Carpenter said. "We were all his family, he cared about us deeply, and we knew he would always be there for us."

Miami of Ohio players were there for Hep at the end as well. On the day of Hoeppner's memorial service in Bloomington, Ind., more than forty former RedHawk players showed up to pay their final respects. Some were famous, like Steelers quarterback Ben Roethlisberger, but most weren't. Several assembled at meeting spots in Ohio the day of the service and carpooled over to Bloomington.

One former player who wouldn't have missed it for the world was Ron Carpenter. "When he passed away, there was no way I wasn't going to be there for his going home party," Carpenter said. "He was always there for me, and I wanted to be there for him, too."

Kent McCullough was happy so many Miami players showed up that day to pay their respects. At the same time, he couldn't help feeling odd at a memorial service for his mentor in the Hoosier State. "He was an Indiana boy, he ended his career at Indiana and I understand that, but he spent almost twenty years at Miami of Ohio, too," McCullough said. "I remember walking into the basketball arena at Indiana thinking that this should really be at Miami because my memories of Coach Hep were all in Oxford.

"At the same time, it was a great service and I thought the people of Indiana really did a nice job honoring him. You could tell the way he impacted so many people there in such a short time. The thing about Coach Hep was that he impacted people wherever he was coaching."

★ ★ ★

Shean Williams will be the first to admit that he had no intentions of attending Miami of Ohio, even when Terry Hoeppner was recruiting him out of high school in Atlanta. Williams was planning visits to Georgia Southern, Western Carolina, Eastern Carolina, Middle Tennessee State and Wake Forest. The only reason he even checked out Miami of Ohio was that he had never been to Ohio and was going to get a flight out of it.

It was a pleasant night in January, 1989 when Williams arrived in Oxford for his visit. When he woke up the next morning, however, it had snowed two to three feet. There was no way he was going to end up at Miami, he thought.

Hoeppner showed up to pick him up, and from that point on everything changed. The first place Hoeppner took him that morning really took him by surprise. "The first thing he did was take me back to his house to meet his family," Williams said. "That's the honest-to-God truth. And I've got to tell you that really impressed me. At the time, his daughter Allison was a senior in high school, so she was the same age as I was. I hung out with all of them for a short while, and you could just see how much joy they had for each other. As I sat there that day, I remember thinking that I'd really like to be around a coach who placed that much importance on his family."

Hoeppner's second stop with Williams that day was to meet the head of the finance department. "He knew I wanted to be a finance major, so that's where we went next," Williams said. "I didn't get to see the football complex until later that afternoon. He showed me what was important first. I knew I was never going to play pro ball so the other things were always important to me. I feel like Hep believed in me as a football player, but most of all as a man." Williams never made those other five recruiting visits. After a snowy weekend with Hoeppner in Ohio, he committed to playing for the RedHawks.

☆ ☆ ☆

When Williams got married on March 9, 2001 in Atlanta, he sent the Hoeppners a wedding invitation, never expecting that they'd come. It had been eight years since he graduated from Miami, and he had already begun practicing law in Georgia.

But the Hoeppners did come to the wedding, and Terry was able to enjoy one of his favorite hobbies on the morning of Williams' wedding. "I turned into a pretty adequate golfer after I left Miami," Williams said. "Hep had always tried to get me to learn to play golf while I was there. He was pretty sure I was never going to play in the NFL, and he figured I'd probably be a lawyer someday. He thought knowing how to play golf would come in handy. And of course he was right."

Shean and Marie-Yolaine Williams' wedding was in the evening, and instead of having a bachelor party, Shean organized a golf outing for his friends the morning of the wedding. The truth is, he invited everybody there – and Hep took over. "Even that day he made a competition of it," Williams said. "He broke us up into teams, and the first group played rabbit or something like that, and the next group played something else. He was really in his element.

"I've got to say that one of my fondest memories of Hep

is him making it to my wedding. But, even better, while he was there he played golf with me, spent the day and evening with us, and celebrated one of the biggest days of my life," Williams said. "The best thing I can say about Hep is that he was always there."

★ ★ ★

Several former Miami players talked about the way Terry Hoeppner motivated them. Many think it was one of his greatest attributes. Dustin Cohen, who was at Miami from 1995-2000, played three years under Randy Walker as the head coach and one season for Hoeppner. When Walker was the head coach, Hep was the defensive coordinator.

"I loved playing for both of those coaches, but Coach Hep made you want to play *for* him instead of in fear of him," Cohen said. "Hep had a way of getting the most out of his players just by being positive. He would never get in your ear about how bad you did. He'd simply look at you and you'd feel horrible, like you let him down. When you played for Coach Hep, you never wanted to let him down."

Kent McCullough, who in 2007 was a graduate assistant coach at the University of Missouri, said the "Don't Quit" poem that Hoeppner was so fond of served as a great motivator for him, and it's something he uses with his players today. "He would get so animated and passionate when he rattled off the words to that poem. Kids of all ages can relate to it," McCullough said. "Every time I hear that poem, I think of Hep, and I know I always will."

★ ★ ★

Ron Carpenter came to Miami of Ohio as a walk-on wide receiver. He had injured his knee prior to his senior year in high school and wasn't recruited heavily because of it. When he arrived in Oxford, he felt he had something to prove.

Hep first thought he was a loud mouth. Carpenter would catch passes against Hoeppner's defensive backs and then start trash talking. Hep found out pretty quickly from the wide receivers coach that Carpenter wasn't in the receiving plans. Because of Carpenter's athleticism, Hep asked the wide receivers coach for permission to move him to defense, where he redshirted him but set him up for the next four years.

Carpenter would go on to start four years as defensive back at Miami and then move on to an NFL career that included stops with Minnesota, Cincinnati, the New York Jets and St. Louis. He ended up playing on the Rams' 1999 Super Bowl championship team.

"I always figured that my best shot at the NFL would be at wide receiver, but Hep saw something different, and I'll be forever grateful to him for that," Carpenter said. "He saw the potential in me and made the switch, and everything worked out great. Looking back, I don't think I ever would have made it to the NFL as a wide receiver. So I have coach Hep to thank for that."

✳ ✳ ✳

To those who knew Hoeppner, Carpenter's story was more the rule than the exception. Hep had the gift of being able to look at a player and determine the best position for him to play. At Indiana, more than a dozen players switched from one side of the ball to the other in his two-plus seasons. That happened frequently at Miami, too.

While many recruited Shean Williams as a wide receiver, Hoeppner had him pegged as a defensive back. Truthfully, many people didn't even see him as a football player. Williams came to Miami of Ohio at 5' 8" and 132 pounds, dripping wet. "This was 1989, and most wide receivers were 5' 10" or 5' 11" and weighed 185 or 190 pounds," Williams said. "Hep saw something in me that I guess everybody else didn't. Everyone else wanted me to play receiver, but he was adamant about me playing corner. I didn't care, I just wanted to play football."

✳ ✳ ✳

Josh Betts has many good memories of playing quarterback for Terry Hoeppner at Miami. He credits Hoeppner for helping him stay focused in the years when he backed up Ben Roethlisberger. Hep had a lot to do with his later success as a starter as well because of his coach's belief in him.

But Betts said the greatest gift Hoeppner gave him was teaching him family values. "Coach Hep and his wife Jane were so good to me in my years at Miami and I'll never forget that," Betts said. "Jane Hoeppner is a wonderful woman, and I'm truly blessed to have gotten to know her in my years at Miami. Both of them taught me the importance of family in difficult times. I had a couple of friends die while I was at Miami, and the Hoeppners were very understanding and helped me through it. They taught me that football was important, but God, faith and family are more important. That's the way Hep lived his life, and I feel like I was lucky just to have gotten to know him as well as I did."

When former Miami player Dustin Cohen was in school, it was cool to refer to your girlfriend or your wife as your "old lady." But Cohen never heard anything close to that from Hoeppner. "All he did was talk about love and respect," Cohen said. "He talked a lot about Mrs. Hoeppner and that was admirable. He didn't hide behind the image that football players were all egocentric, tough men. He was real, and I think that resonated favorably with a lot of guys as well."

★ ★ ★

Of all the things that Martin Nance experienced while playing for Terry Hoeppner at Miami of Ohio from 2000-04, one of his most memorable was getting a first-hand look at Hep's magical remedy for healing just about any kind of athletic injury. Talk to any player who played for Hep at either Miami or Indiana, and you'll hear the same story over and over. For Hep, it was all about ice and the hot tub. Coach Hep routinely invited players to his house during the week in big groups to sit around and watch football and eventually undergo "treatment."

Hep swore that any injury could be healed by icing it down, sitting in the hot tub, then icing it down again. The sequence should be repeated as often as necessary. "I remember one time I had a really sore ankle, and I was struggling at practice during the week. Coach Hep came up to me at the end of practice and suggested I stop by his house later that night and bring my swimsuit," Nance said. "When I got there, I joined several of my teammates already in the hot tub. When we got out we iced our injuries down. The most amazing part of it all, though, is it worked just the way Coach Hep told me it would. That Saturday, when I got up in the morning, my ankle felt a lot better, and I went out and had a big game against the University of Cincinnati." Nance smiled through the telephone as he recounted that story. "Coach Hep had some healing powers. I know that for sure."

When Hoeppner recruited Nance out of St. Louis, he dangled a huge carrot in front of the wide receiver. If Nance chose Miami, he'd get to play with a guy named Roethlisberger. The coach told him being on the receiving end of Roethlisberger's passes could be just what Nance needed to have a shot at playing on Sundays. "I remember meeting Ben on my recruiting visit and finally putting a face with all the things Coach Hep had been telling me about him," Nance said. "But he was right. Roethlisberger and I had some good years together, and I have to credit Coach Hep with making it happen." With both Roethlisberger and Hep's help, Nance did go on to play as a wide receiver in the NFL. In both 2006 and 2007, Nance was with the Minnesota Vikings.

The last time Nance saw his college coach was at the Super Bowl in Detroit following the 2005 season. Hoeppner, just one month after his first brain surgery, was there to see Roethlisberger and the Steelers. "When I look back on that day, all I remember about Hep is how great he looked and how he said he felt better than he had in a long, long time," Nance said. "And all I could think of was that this guy just had brain surgery, and this was his outlook on life. It made me have an even higher opinion of Coach Hep. He looked so good that day that I never had any doubts he could find a way to beat brain cancer."

Chapter 13
Dr. Adam Herbert

In one of the first conversations he had with Terry Hoeppner, IU president Dr. Adam Herbert shared his concerns about the kinds of football players Indiana was recruiting. Ever since he came on board at IU in August of 2003, Herbert noticed one thing in particular about Indiana's offensive and defensive linemen: They weren't very big. Herbert's point was this – You're never going to be successful in the Big Ten if you don't have linemen bigger than the university president. Herbert is 6' 4" and tips the scales around 255 or 260.

Hearing that observation, Hoeppner nodded his head in agreement. "You know, you may be on to something there," Hoeppner told him. It also made Hep that much more aware of the president's size. In fact, he gave Herbert a nickname that day, the "Big Bear."

Herbert remembers talking to Hoeppner some time after Hep put together a recruiting class with seven offensive linemen he affectionately named the "seven blocks of limestone." That group averaged 6' 6" and 290 pounds. "He called me and told me about the class he had assembled," Herbert recalled. "And one of his big points to me was, 'We've got some fellas here who are bigger than the Big Bear.'"

✫ ✫ ✫

Herbert vividly remembers the interview sessions with each of the candidates brought in for the head coaching job in December of 2004. The president had a total of five interviews, with each lasting close to three hours. The process took a day and a half. "It was very clear to all of us that Hep was the one we wanted to hire," Herbert said. "He had all the things we were looking for in a coach, and he really made the process pretty easy."

One of Herbert's memories of the interview with Hoeppner was the way Hep sat on the sofa that day. At no point did Hoeppner's back ever come in contact with the back of the sofa. "He sat forward the whole time and was so animated," Herbert said. "He had such a passion for the university and the football job that frankly energized everyone in that room. From that moment on he maintained that energy level. I think the greatest compliment I could pay to Terry Hoeppner is I can honestly tell you that Hep exceeded my very high expectations for the next football coach. And for me, that's saying something."

★ ★ ★

Herbert and Hoeppner didn't have your typical president/football coach relationship. Hoeppner once told Herbert that he had never had the kind of relationship with a president that the two of them were able to share. They talked every week, sometimes several times. They discussed football, but that wasn't always the focus of their conversations. They were both avid readers and talked at length about the titles they were currently reading. Herbert might stop by Hep's office just to say hello and wind up sitting there for twenty to thirty minutes wrapped up in conversation. Herbert referred to those moments as being "Hepped." When it came to conversation, Hoeppner was never concerned with brevity.

Herbert was proud of his atypical relationship with his football coach. "I think one of the things you find with a lot of college presidents is that they don't want to be that closely associated with athletics for political reasons," Herbert said. "When I came to the university, in talking with the board of

Opposite page: Coach Hoeppner looks concerned in a 2006 road game.

trustees, one of the things that was clear was that we had major problems in athletics that had to be fixed. Some of that had to do with the budget situation, and some of it was in other areas."

Herbert monitored athletics closely right from the start. He wanted the department to know they had the support of the president's office, and made it clear that turning the football program around, and ultimately having the right man in place to do that, was Job One.

"In the case of Coach Hoeppner, one thing that made it easier for me was that he and I shared so many values," Herbert said. "We also really enjoyed talking with each other and I think that made a difference as well. I talked to him on the phone at home, and I'd sit in the coach's box from time to time, and that gave me a clearer sense of what was going on with IU football. It gave me an opportunity to be supportive of Coach Hep and his players."

★ ★ ★

Herbert remembers Hoeppner as a man of integrity who kept his promises. In the final conversation that he and IU athletic director Rick Greenspan had with Hoeppner before offering him the job, Hep gave a very specific outline of things that needed to be done moving forward. Then he went out and did them.

He had the plan, and as he quickly showed Herbert, he worked the plan, too. "His vision for what needed to be done was very clear," Herbert said. "In that final conversation before we offered him the position, we talked about "The Rock." We talked about "The Walk" and about his intentions of going around the state to talk to alumni. We talked about his feelings toward the students and how he was going to reach out to them in a way that had not been done for many years here. Everything that he said needed to be done, he went out and did."

★ ★ ★

When Herbert looks back on his time with Hoeppner, he'll remember the good times, the big wins, the way Hep worked a crowd and the limitless devotion for his family. But what he'll remember the most is the way Hoeppner handled adversity.

Herbert was with the IU football team in November of 2006 when they headed to Minnesota to play a game that could have put the Hoosiers at the magical six victory plateau, thus giving them elusive bowl eligibility. With recent victories over Iowa and Michigan State, optimism was high as IU headed to the Metrodome to face a struggling Golden Gophers team. While it wasn't shocking that Minnesota won the game, what was surprising was the way the Gophers manhandled the Hoosiers. Minnesota jumped out to a 35-0 lead in the second quarter and won going away, 62-26.

Herbert described his coach as being "extremely disappointed" as the team left Minnesota that day. But like he always did with his team, he tried to spin it positively and looked ahead. "We've still got two more chances at this thing," Hep said. "This is a setback, but it's not something we can't overcome. Our goal of playing thirteen games this season is still alive."

"He always had the right words to motivate, inspire and build confidence," Herbert said. "He stressed that you could overcome anything. That these were temporary barriers. Even after we lost to Michigan and Purdue to end the season, he was finding ways to put it in a positive light. He talked about that season laying the foundation for going to a bowl game next season."

Herbert saw that optimism manifested in his fight against brain cancer, too. "He was always so upbeat and convinced that in the end he was going to win," Herbert said. "And I don't think there was anyone who knew him who didn't believe that was exactly what he was going to do."

Chapter 14
Competitive Edge

It's unclear if Terry Hoeppner loved to win or just hated to lose. Regardless, his friends and colleagues will tell you that Hoeppner was one of the most competitive people they ever met. It didn't matter what the sport was. It didn't even need to *be* a sport. If there was a way to compete, Hep wanted to be part of it – and he wanted to win, too.

Any time the coaching staff got together socially, the coaches were expected to bring their wives and kids to the gathering. They also knew to expect some kind of competition as well, with Hep right in the middle of it. "There was always a game going on, with something on the line," said assistant coach Brian George. "And you could always count on it being competitive."

One year for the staff Christmas party everyone went bowling. Hoeppner paired up the two-person teams with a coach and a wife, but spouses weren't paired together. "So we're out bowling and Courtney Palcic is absolutely mortified," George recalled. "I think she and Joe were still engaged at the time, and she was scared to death she would get paired up with Hep, and that she would be the reason they lost. Her fear didn't come true, but Hep did hate to lose, there was no doubt about that."

The games were constantly changing, but the competition was always the same. They played bocce, ring toss, corn hole or any number of games. "Don't get me wrong, as coaches we loved to compete with him because competition is a big part of what we do," George said. "But our wives would just look at us and shake their heads, wondering, 'Can't we just go out to dinner or something?'"

☆ ☆ ☆

Assistant coach Billy Lynch always thought he was competitive, until he met Terry Hoeppner. "People have always told me, that almost to a fault, I'm too competitive. But I wasn't half as competitive as Hep," Billy Lynch said. He remembers competing with Hep, on both sides of the ledger.

On Signing Day at Miami, the coaching staff used to go to the Hole in the Wall pizza place. They had a shuffle-board-style game there that Hoeppner and his partner, strength and conditioning coach Dan Dalrymple, always won. This particular year, however, a couple of graduate assistants, Billy Lynch and Craig Aukerman, played Hep and Dalrymple and beat them.

"We ended up beating them, and I remember everybody saying, 'What in the hell are you doing?'" Lynch said. "I was a first year G.A., and maybe I was even talking some trash. I think deep down Hep respected us and appreciated that we were going right at him, but at the same time he was so mad."

Lynch also remembers a ring toss game that Hoeppner set up in his backyard at Oxford. The idea was to toss your rings onto the pegs. Hep thought Billy would be really good at it because it required just the right touch, and Billy had played a lot of basketball growing up. Hep was wrong, and Billy sure heard about it.

"I was the worst player ever to play that game," Billy Lynch said. "And Hep was very agitated because he figured I'd be so good. I couldn't get one of them on. He was so mad, I remember him yelling, 'Are you kidding me?' He could be your best friend if you were doing well, but man he could turn on you, too. He was fun to play with, though, especially if you were doing well."

When Miami played Louisville in the 2003 GMAC Bowl in Mobile, Ala., the two teams competed against each other in other activities leading up to the game. One night there was a bowling match between the two teams, another night was a cheer competition, and the game itself was on the third night. Hep was fired up about beating Louisville every night that week and was going around trying to pump everybody up for the bowling match first.

"Our starting safety Steve Burke was bowling about a fifty-three through five frames when Hep stopped him and told him to 'get out of there,'" Lynch said. "Burke's bowling shoes were two sizes smaller than Hep's, but Hep told him to take them off, and he squeezed into them anyway. So Hep bowled because he wanted to make sure we beat them at bowling before we played our game."

Lynch doesn't remember who won the bowling; however, chances are pretty good that Hoeppner remembered who had won – and probably the score. Regardless, everyone at Miami remembered the outcome of the football game: Miami 49, Louisville 28.

✮ ✮ ✮

Assistant coach Joe Palcic recalls Hoeppner boasting about his "victories" in staff meetings. "He would tell us stories in private and say, 'Yeah, last night at home, me and Jane, the kids and the grandkids were playing a board game,' and he'd add, 'and I kicked her (butt).' He wouldn't let his wife beat him in a board game, that's how competitive the guy was. It was almost comical. 'I'm not going to let Jane beat me at anything,' Hep would say."

For the record, Jane Hoeppner was fond of bringing up the fact that she had the upper hand against her husband in miniature golf. "That's not a real sport," Coach would say. She also held her own in Trivial Pursuit, eventually leading her husband to stop playing the game.

✮ ✮ ✮

Assistant coach Bobby Johnson first got to know Hep well in the summer of 1992, following his freshman season as a player at Miami of Ohio. It was a competitive situation that got the two acquainted.

Johnson stayed at Miami that summer to lift weights and attend summer school, and he and several of his Miami teammates played on a slow-pitch softball team. The idea was to find an activity where they could have some fun, let off some steam, and get to know each other better. There was one assistant coach who played on the team as well. Yes, Hoeppner played third base, and he played to win.

It was an eye-opening experience – that is, for the two or three games that Hep actually played that season. "He was our third baseman and our best player," Johnson recalled. "He didn't quite make it the full season because he broke his wrist sliding into third trying to take the extra base. He finished that game, but didn't play anymore.

"Here we were, eighteen- and nineteen-year-old kids, all Division I college athletes, and here's this coach who is a lot older than we are, and he was better than all of us. It wasn't even close. We were all thinking, 'This will be a little summer fun for us,' but he was going all out. That was my first real glimpse of Hep as a person and not just a football coach."

⋆ ⋆ ⋆

Of all the games Hep loved away from the football field, none was more important than golf. Golf was Hoeppner's passion, and he played in the offseason as much as time allowed. He had a net in his garage where he'd hit hundreds and hundreds of golf balls.

His average score was Red Grange, a 77 (Grange's uniform number). "If I can shoot Red Grange, I'm happy," Hoeppner once said. His best round ever was a 68 in 2002 at Liberty Country Club in Liberty, Ind.

It's been said that everyone who knew Terry Hoeppner has a Hep story. A large number of those involve golf. "He was very competitive, I'll tell you that," said assistant coach Matt Canada. "He wanted to win. If he wasn't playing well, he was upset. And if he was winning, he told you that he was kicking your tail. But it was fun. From where I stood, three things were really important to Hep: Football, family and golf. And he was very active in all three."

The coaching staff accompanied Hoeppner on many golf outings during the summer. But as much as Hep enjoyed getting out and talking to alumni, he wasn't crazy about golf outings because they were often scrambles. Hep liked to play his own ball. "If you're a ragged golfer, scrambles are a lot of fun," Canada said. "But if you're a good golfer like Hep, it was probably the opposite."

Hoeppner once told the *Indianapolis Star* that he played in way too many scrambles. "Playing in scrambles really makes it hard, especially with my putting," Hoeppner said. "Part of my putting trouble is I need three people to putt first before I can putt."

There was a lot of pressure on coaches that got paired up with Hoeppner at golf events, particularly if there was money on the line (no matter how small the amount). "If you were playing with Hep, you didn't want to be having a bad day, I'll tell you that," Palcic said.

Billy Lynch remembers one of those days on the golf course. Billy's "baseball grip" swing style became a point of contention the last time Billy and Hep were partners. Billy Lynch has been known to be able to get a hold of his drives, but because of his grip he'll often duck hook it. "I was nervous, and I was trying to kill it, and I just kept duck hooking it," Billy Lynch said. "Finally, Hep told me, 'Unless you get that grip fixed, I'm never playing with you again.' I'll tell you this, though, as partners we won a lot. I'm only telling you the times he was mad at me because they're a little more humorous."

The first few months Shane Montgomery, who was on Hoeppner's staff at Miami and later succeeded him as head coach, was in Oxford in 2001 Hoeppner showed him around town, always making a stop at Oxford Country Club. "I remember him dragging me out to the putting green and having competitions over lunch," Montgomery said. "It was always the same. We would play for who was going to buy lunch. And I remember thinking, 'Man, this guy is a competitor. He's got me out here the first couple of weeks and he's trying to win lunch from me.' But that was just who Hep, was and it was all part of his charm."

☆ ☆ ☆

When Bill Lynch Sr. was the head football coach at Ball State, and Hoeppner was the head man at Miami, the two friends started a home-and-away golf tournament to be used for bragging rights. One weekend the site would be the Delaware Country Club in Muncie, and the next the Oxford Country Club in Oxford, Ohio. Both groups would bring two foursomes for the competition.

"We would try to bring as many ringers as we could," Bill Lynch recalls of the event. "One year I brought one of our associate athletic directors, who just happened to be a scratch golfer, and another time I actually brought our golf coach with us."

Lynch remembers one trip to Oxford when Hoeppner, on a long par 4, hit a 3-iron onto the green. "It was a blind shot, up over a hill, and Hep knocked this little field shot in there. When we got up there we couldn't find it anywhere," Lynch said, "and sure enough, it was in the hole. He didn't let us forget that one anytime soon. In fact, I think every time I played with him he mentioned that shot."

One year in Muncie, Hoeppner chose Montgomery, his offensive coordinator, as his partner. Montgomery is a good golfer, but he and Hoeppner were no match for the group that Lynch put together that day. "We may have had a ringer that day," Lynch said with a sly smile.

The next week, they came back to Oxford to play and Montgomery was busy. The only guy available to play was Joe Palcic – and he was nervous. "I got drafted when Shane couldn't play, and let me tell you it was serious," Palcic said. "It was The Masters. The pressure was on me. There was no way Hep was going to lose back-to-back matches. I played

OK, and we actually won that one, but I remember the pressure and thinking all day long what it would be like if we didn't win."

★ ★ ★

Franklin College football coach Mike Leonard worked several summer camps with Terry Hoeppner, during which he got to know long-time Franklin coach Red Faught very well. Faught and Hoeppner were very close, and Faught loved to tell stories about Hoeppner's competitive side. Leonard heard second hand on more than one occasion about some of the times that Faught and Hoeppner would sneak away during spring practice to try and play 18 holes at Hillview Country Club in Franklin late in the day.

"Red always talked about how they'd play a round of golf, and Hep might have a couple of bad holes that would ruin his whole round," Leonard said. "And so they'd be finishing up and as they headed to the parking lot Hep would tell Coach Faught, 'You know what, I'm staying. I'm going to beat this thing.' And Hep would head back out on the course for more. He may have had sixteen good holes, but one or two got him that shouldn't have, and he was going back to get 'em. I've never been that driven about something like that. But hearing the story it certainly didn't surprise me that it might be the case with Coach Hep."

While Leonard's stories of Hoeppner on the golf course were second hand, former Indiana Alumni Association President Ken Beckley got to see it all up close and personal at several alumni golf outings. He remembered one in particular, when he was in Hoeppner's foursome. Beckley had never played with him before and had no idea how competitive the IU coach was on the golf course. On the first tee, Hoeppner hit a good tee shot, long and straight, right down the middle. Beckley's shot wasn't quite as perfect. He hit a draw that was almost a hook and did not fill Coach Hep with a great deal of confidence. "He just stared at me, and I thought, 'Oh my gosh, I'm in for it today,'" Beckley said. "And it was just because he wanted to win that tournament. He wanted our foursome to do well. He didn't just play for the fun of it. If he didn't have a chance to win, he wasn't having fun."

Later in that round, Beckley got to witness what happened when Hep got *really* intense. There was a very small stream maybe three feet wide in front of the hole, and Hoeppner had to chip over that to the green. He proceeded to chunk his shot and the ball went in the water. But that wasn't all that got wet. In an instant, Hoeppner's pitching wedge followed the golf ball into the stream. "There wasn't enough water there to carry the club down stream or anything, and he was able to reach in and get it, but you could see from that moment that he really had the passion to win. It was just a golf scramble with alumni, certainly not anything major, but that didn't matter to him. It was a sporting event and he didn't want to lose. I know a lot of people saw that side of him with football, but I saw it on the golf course, too."

☆ ☆ ☆

Don Fischer, the long-time Indiana football broadcaster, can be a tad-bit competitive on the golf course as well. And like Hep, Fischer was always looking for anything that might give him an edge. In late December of 2006, Hoeppner was over at Fischer's home for a party, and the two went down to the basement so Fish could show him where he hit golf balls. The hitting area, off to one side of the basement, has a mat from which he hits golf balls into a net. "Well, Hep didn't like the mat," Fischer said. 'I've got a better thing than that called a Par Buster,' Hep said. It was a mat with springs underneath it that 'gave' like you're hitting off the ground. He told me, 'Man, with this set up you're screwing up your elbows when you hit the ball. Besides that, you don't have the same feel that you'd get from hitting off the ground.'"

The next day, Fischer and Hoeppner met at Bloomington Country Club for a round of golf. The night before Hep told Fish that he would bring the Par Buster with him so he could demonstrate how it worked. "After the round, as we were walking out to the cars, I asked him if he had remembered to bring the Par Buster. And he went to his SUV, got out this Par Buster, and I'm telling you this thing was probably four feet long by two feet wide, and it was on springs and it was heavy. He took it out and set it on the ground, and we hit clubs on it for probably forty minutes.'"

After they were finished, Fischer told him "Coach, I've got to get one of these," and the next day he went out and ordered one. Within a month it was in his basement. "And I called him and told him I had it, and he said, 'Isn't that the greatest thing you've ever seen?' He loved golf. He had a set up in his garage like I had in my basement, where he hit hundreds of balls into a net. But he was so proud of his Par Buster and now was proud that he'd shown it to me and I had gone out and bought one. Now in his mind I was some-how part of the club. But I'll never forget how happy he was showing me how his toy worked."

Chapter 15
Never Met a Stranger

Terry Hoeppner didn't just touch the lives of coaches, players, administrators and close friends. Whether it was a brief conversation at a Kiwanis Club meeting or an introduction at a golf outing or pancake breakfast, Hoeppner's engaging style left a mark on people every day. He simply had the gift of connecting with people and making them feel comfortable.

The list of those with Hep memories is long. Some knew Hep well; others perhaps only had that chance conversation. The common bond in all the stories is that knowing Terry Hoeppner made people's lives better. Who wouldn't love to have that said about them?

☆ ☆ ☆

Indiana State Police trooper Curt Durnil headed the police detail that escorted IU to games, both home and away, and became close friends with Hoeppner and his family. A Durnil tradition is the annual college football kickoff party at his home. He invites all of the Indiana football detail state troopers and sometimes the support personnel as well. One year, he also dropped off an invitation to Hoeppner's office, never believing for a minute that the IU head coach would stop by his party. But he wanted to let the coaches know that they were welcome to attend.

"Well, about a half hour into it this guy walks up my steps, and I ask my dad who it is. He tells me it's Coach

Hoeppner," Durnil said. "I was like, 'Are you kidding me?' But no, he drove out to my house by himself. He had never been there before, but he came to my football party. And he didn't just make an appearance and leave. He stayed there, joked with us, and helped himself to the barbeque wings that I had. Then he went into my boys' bedrooms and signed their 'Coach Hep Wants You' posters.

"He was one of the guys. I couldn't believe it. Situations like that added to his legacy with us. He's a Division I head coach. He's not supposed to have time for stuff like that. But Hep made time. And that's what set him apart."

☆ ☆ ☆

Indiana Governor Mitch Daniels had the pleasure of meeting Terry and Jane Hoeppner on a couple of occasions. He remembers his first conversation with Hep just a few days after he took the Indiana job in December of 2004. Daniels called him as a fan, and told him he was excited Hoeppner was coming to Indiana and if there was anything he could do for Hep he would like to do it.

"He was already in promotion mode," Daniels said. "He wanted me to come to the spring game and call a play. I've always regretted that I had a conflict that day and couldn't do it, but I remember hanging up the phone and thinking, 'This guy is going to be great.' He was barely in the saddle, and he was already thinking up ways to get people excited about the program."

Another memory involved an RV that Daniels took around the state as an opportunity to meet the citizens of Indiana. One fall weekend he took the RV to Memorial Stadium and was tailgating just as Hep and the Indiana team walked by during the "Walk to the Rock."

"When the team started coming, I went out with the crowd and was kind of standing there in the mob off to one side as everyone started parading past. I called his name and waved to him, and he hustled over, jerked me out into the middle of the walk, and asked me to walk with him. He started asking me questions about something we were working hard on at the time, like balancing the budget. He wanted to know about this and that, and I'm thinking, 'Hey Coach, you should be focusing on the game and not on me.' I walked with him for two or three blocks until I was finally able to break loose and get into the open field. But he was just irrepressible. And I know he was that way with everyone."

☆ ☆ ☆

IU basketball coach Kelvin Sampson didn't have a long time to get to know Terry Hoeppner, but one thing that always stood out was the importance he placed on supporting other programs within the athletic department. He took his team to volleyball games the night before football games to show support. He was visible at soccer games, too.

And of course there was basketball. Hoeppner was an IU hoops fan long before he was the Indiana head coach, and he enjoyed going to games or using IU basketball as an opportunity to entertain recruits. Sampson remembers the January 31, 2007 game against Wisconsin at Assembly Hall. Unranked Indiana knocked off No. 2 Wisconsin that night, 71-66.

"It was apparent with about fifty seconds to go that the students were going to rush the court when the game was over," Sampson said. "So I started thinking about an exit strategy. (Wisconsin coach) Bo Ryan is a good friend of mine, and I wanted to make sure I went down and told him how much I respected him and the way his team played, too. So I did that, and when I turned back, the kids were pouring out on the floor. I did some running high fives as I tried to get back to the locker room. Once I got clear, I made a mad dash to that locker room entrance, and some guy jumped right out in front of me and extended his arms to give me an embrace."

It was Terry Hoeppner.

"He's got his baseball cap on and the biggest, widest grin, and he has both arms out. And he says, 'Way to go, baby. Great job!' And we hugged. I think it was neat that he felt it was important enough to come down and share that moment with me. All Hep ever wanted was for IU athletic programs to do well."

⋆ ⋆ ⋆

Kelly Bomba is an associate director for the IU Varsity Club. Her husband Matt is a former Indiana football player (1988-92) and former strength and conditioning coach for the Hoosiers. Her dad Bob Van Pelt played for the Hoosiers from 1964-67, and her father-in-law Brad Bomba played football at IU from 1953-57 and was an All-American selection for the Hoosiers in 1956. Brad Bomba was also a former team physician for the IU basketball team. In other words, IU football is in the family's blood.

Apparently it hasn't skipped any generations either, as Matt and Kelly's nearly 6-year-old son James has a Hep memory of his own.

"On my fourth birthday, my mom took me to Coach Hep's Monday night radio show," James Bomba said. "He gave me a red bracelet like the team wore and he even wished me happy birthday on the air. That was pretty cool."

Sometimes James would draw Coach Hep pictures or send him notes when he was sick. "I prayed for him every night – sometimes twice." When he found out Hep died James was very sad. He told his mom he figured Coach Hep was up in heaven talking about IU football with Mo (former IU football player, Yernonimo Ciriaco, who was killed in a car accident in 2004.) "I got a nice note from Mrs. Hoeppner with a very special gift – one of Coach Hep's whistles," James Bomba said. "I will take good care of that whistle because it will always remind me of my good friend."

⋆ ⋆ ⋆

Brenda and Ken Roethlisberger, parents of former Miami quarterback Ben Roethlisberger, thought for the longest time that their son had a one-in-a-million relationship with his college coach Terry Hoeppner. They just figured that he had gotten lucky and had something with this man that few other people got to experience.

When they attended Hoeppner's memorial service in June of 2007, however, they realized how wrong they had been. "When we were at the funeral and we heard all of these stories and saw all of these young men who had been touched by Hep, we realized that Ben had been one of many," Brenda Roethlisberger said. "But he made Ben, and he made us, feel like Ben was the only one. And I think now that he probably did that for just about everyone."

☆ ☆ ☆

Mike MacDonald and Ben Oprinovich were seniors at Indiana hoping to graduate in the spring of 2008. Both were deeply touched by Terry Hoeppner in his short time at IU. A few months after Hep died, the students decided to print T-shirts saying "WIN IT FOR HEP." They wanted to sell them to Bloomington residents and IU students for $10 each and donate all the profits to the North End Zone Project at Memorial Stadium. One of Hoeppner's visions at IU was to see the stadium and the football facilities get properly renovated.

"The first year Coach Hep was here we had the 'Coach Hep Wants You' posters (the cover photo on this book), and now after he's gone we still have 'Play 13' and 'Win It for Hep,'" MacDonald said. "His legacy continues to live on. I think students are confident that this team is going to play in a bowl game, and it's unfortunate that he can't be on the sideline coaching us, but I think most everyone agrees that he's in a better seat."

☆ ☆ ☆

Dawn Clark, as a secretary in the football office, had the pleasure of working with Terry Hoeppner for all nineteen of his seasons at Miami of Ohio. She remembers that Coach Hep wasn't a big computer guy. "He might check his e-mail or go online to print out an article on an opponent, but that was about it," she said.

One day during preseason, Hoeppner was having computer difficulties. She could hear him banging loudly on the keys, but she had learned from working with multiple head coaches that there were times to intervene and times to leave the coach alone. This was an instance where she definitely did not want to intervene. "Just when I was thinking, 'Uh-oh,' he walked out and tossed the laptop in the garbage can. I had to snicker to myself as he opened the door and walked down the hall in a fit of rage. Five minutes later, he was back, fishing it out of the garbage can, and it was everything I could do to not laugh hysterically."

☆ ☆ ☆

In 2007 Joe Smith was about to begin his twenty-fifth season with the IU Football Network. He has handled pre-game, halftime and post game duties since 1983. During that time he's seen coaches come and go, but he had a fondness for Coach Hep that he found difficult to put into words.

"Hep always made time for me, and that's what I'll remember the most," Smith said. "He didn't have to do it. I had some scheduling conflicts, and the only time I could meet him was on Thursday afternoons. But he always agreed to do it. We would meet in his office or in the meeting room and I'd do the interview. Sometimes we'd talk about life. Sometimes we'd talk about family. And sometimes we would even talk about football. But as a local sports guy, he always took time for me, and that's something I'll never forget."

☆ ☆ ☆

Dick Dullaghan is recognized as one of the greatest Indiana high school football coaches of all time. He has won eight Indiana state high school football championships and in 1991 was named the national coach of the year. Terry Hoeppner worked his football camps, dating all the way back to when Hep was an assistant coach at Franklin College. Dullaghan admired his passion and enthusiasm.

Dullaghan remembers how excited the state high school coaching fraternity was in 2004 when Indiana hired Hoeppner as its new head coach. "If you were a football guy in Indiana, you knew Terry Hoeppner," Dullaghan said. "He had been a high school coach in Indiana, he coached Franklin College in the state, and he had recruited Indiana well in the years he was at Miami. Every coach in Indiana knew if he sent his kid to Hep, it was going to be good for the kid. The kid was going to enjoy playing the game he loved, and he was going to play for a man who cared about him long after he stopped playing football."

★ ★ ★

Mark Deal, an assistant director at the IU Varsity Club, first met Terry Hoeppner in 1980. Hep was the linebackers coach at Franklin College, and Deal was the linebackers coach at Wabash.

"At the small-college level you do everything," Deal said. "You carry the dummies from the shed to the field, drive the vans to the games, line the fields, help with the uniform laundry, pretty much you name it. Also we all coached a spring sport, and coaches always helped out if one of the other sports was holding a spring tournament."

Deal remembers going to Franklin College on a cold, rainy day for the Little State track meet. There was Hoeppner running the shot put competition on a wet, muddy field. "I remember Hep running the event and encouraging the competitors at the same time," Deal said. "He was a ray of sunshine on a forty-degree, rainy Indiana spring day."

★ ★ ★

When Indiana associate athletic director Kit Klingelhoffer thinks about Terry Hoeppner, he always goes instantly to a story Hoeppner told reporters the day he was hired as the IU football coach. Hep was asked if he was a big IU basketball fan, and Hoeppner responded that he was. "I remember him talking about watching the 1987 NCAA championship game on television. He got so excited when Keith Smart hit the shot to win the game that he pulled a muscle in his leg leaping over his couch in celebration," Klingelhoffer said. "I thought to myself, 'This guy was at Miami then, but he was still a Hoosier.' That story always brings a smile to my face."

★ ★ ★

Governor Mitch Daniels and his wife Sherry make it a point every once in a while to invite people they feel are important in the state's life to a dinner at the Governor's residence. On March 12, 2007, they invited Jane and Terry Hoeppner. Unfortunately, Hep's health had taken a turn that week and the Hoeppners had to pass on the invitation.

Daniels later got a wonderful note from Jane in which she expressed regret that they were unable to attend the dinner, but was hopeful that they would have the opportunity to get together with the Governor and his wife at a future date. She sent the note within a few days of the dinner, but for some reason it got sent to the wrong place, and Daniels didn't actually see it until July, a few weeks after Hoeppner died.

Along with the note, Jane sent the Governor a small replica of "The Rock," one of the most visible symbols of Hoeppner's legacy. "I have it right across from the desk in my office, and it sits in a place of honor right next to a signed basketball from the Milan High School team that inspired the movie *Hoosiers*. I've also got a signed football from Peyton Manning and a few other things. But right in the center is "The Rock" and that's where it's always going to stay.

"My biggest regret, and I hear this from people everywhere I go around the state, is simply that we didn't get to have Terry Hoeppner around for a longer period of time. Like everyone else, I'm thankful for the time we had, but it was just way too short."

Opposite page: Coach Hep is working his plan with Indiana governor Mitch Daniels during "The Walk" to the Rock.

Chapter 16
The Stories Never End

Dave Martz, the long-time athletic director at Eastbrook High School in Marion Ind., was the freshman coach at Eastbrook in the early 1970s, when Terry Hoeppner was the head coach. It was Hoeppner's first coaching job after graduating from Franklin College. One of the things Martz knew right away was that Hoeppner wouldn't be at Eastbrook for very long. "You knew back then he was destined for greatness," Martz said. "There was just something about him."

Martz has a couple of favorite Hoeppner stories. Back then, the paint machine they used to line the field would constantly get clogged. One day Hoeppner and the Eastbrook athletic director were fiddling with it when the new agriculture teacher walked up and asked if he could be of assistance. He was wearing a sport coat, tie and brand new dress shoes. "This young teacher from Purdue walks up, and he's looking at it like he's going to fix it," Martz said. He asked Hoeppner what was the problem, and Hep told him it was clogged and wouldn't paint. At the same time Hep brought the handle up, giving it another quick squeeze to demonstrate the problem. Well, what he didn't realize was that somehow he and the athletic director had fixed the clog, and white paint sprayed out of the machine and all over the teacher's new shoes. "We were rolling on the ground laughing, and this new teacher didn't think it was funny at all," Martz said. "In fact, I think it was probably a month before he spoke to Hep again. Hep felt bad, but not *that* bad."

Martz also remembers Hoeppner at the time was still playing semi-professional football for the Indianapolis Caps out on 16th Street at the CYO fields. "He'd jump in the car after practice on Tuesday and head to Indianapolis to practice with the Caps, and then he'd play in games on Saturday," Martz said. "So he was an active coach with the kids. He would run wind sprints with them at the end of practice. I remember the kids saying they were pretty sure they were always going to have to run because Hep was always running with them."

In 2003, Martz and Rick Atkinson, who was on Hep's staff at Eastbrook, attended a Miami-Ball State game in Muncie. Hoeppner had arranged for the two to be on the sidelines, and they watched as the RedHawks won a lopsided game that day. Late in the fourth quarter, Hoeppner took Ben Roethlisberger out and inserted Josh Betts into the game at quarterback. During a timeout, Hoeppner looked down at Martz and Atkinson and said "What do you guys think we should call here?"

Back in the Eastbrook days, the playbook featured the pass-oriented offense that Hoeppner had played at Franklin College, and the two coaches remembered the terminology. "So Atkinson yells down at Hoeppner, 'Run Wagon Train East,' and I'm yelling, 'No, run Popcorn Trap.' And I'll tell you what, the players were all laughing like they had heard those terms before, and I guess it wouldn't surprise us if they had."

✮ ✮ ✮

Ned Pfau is one of Indiana University's biggest donors and has supported IU athletics for more than forty years. He's had football season tickets since 1965 and basketball season tickets since the first season Bob Knight coached the Hoosiers in 1971. Like most people at Indiana, he only knew Terry Hoeppner a short time, but he was deeply affected by that association.

One of Pfau's favorite Hep stories comes from a trip to New York City he and Hoeppner took in December of 2005 to attend the National Hall of Fame football dinner at the Waldorf Astoria. Hep had asked if he'd like to go with him, and Pfau happily accepted. During the day, Hoeppner and Pfau jogged around Manhattan. Just prior to the dinner they went back to the New York Athletic Club and used the locker room area to change into their tuxedos for the dinner.

As Hoeppner was taking off his pants, Pfau noticed Hoeppner's belt had a nice IU logo on the buckle. He asked him where he got it, and Hoeppner responded, "You like it?" Pfau did and wondered where he could get one. So Hep said, "Well, you can have mine." He pulled it right out of his pants and handed it to Pfau. "I only wear that belt for special occasions and I really cherish it," Pfau said. "But that's just the kind of guy Terry Hoeppner was. If he had something he could give to you, he wouldn't hesitate. He was always thinking about other people."

Pfau recalls one of the last times he saw Hoeppner at an IU basketball game in the spring of 2007. Hep walked up to him and handed him a card he just had printed. One side of the card read "Play 13" with a drawing of a rose. On the other side was one of Hep's favorite sayings: "If you think you can, or you think you can't, you're right." "He was very proud of that card and was already starting to plan ahead. That's one of the hardest parts about moving forward. You have a good feeling that the fruits of his labor will be delivered, but it just makes you ache inside knowing that he won't be there to enjoy it with his staff, players and family."

✭ ✭ ✭

Darcy Shriver works with the Miami of Ohio Alumni Association. She worked closely with the Miami athletic department for all nineteen years that Terry Hoeppner was in Oxford. Like so many others who knew Hep, she said it was impossible to narrow her memories down to just a few stories. But she did have one favorite from 1999, when Hoeppner asked her to be the mistress of ceremonies at the Miami football banquet.

He thought the event could use a little sense of humor and felt she would be the perfect person for the job. Since then, Shriver has served as the M.C. every year. Before the banquet, Coach Hep and Shriver sat down and discussed all the event particulars. He told her he wanted the banquet to end with the fight song, with his 6-year-old grandson, Tucker, leading it. "At the end of the banquet he called Tucker up and put him on a chair, saying, 'We're going to do the fight song on three.' All of these big guys stood up and sang the fight song together.

"That was Terry Hoeppner. First he teaches this young boy the fight song, and then he stands him up in front of 350 people at this banquet. Tucker was wonderful, and we did that every year. It turned out to be a real emotional time. And as the grandchildren got bigger, he brought all of them up to take part. It was a real special time, and he found a way to include his family in that moment."

★ ★ ★

John Pont has a unique perspective when it comes to Terry Hoeppner. Pont, like Hoeppner and former IU coach Bill Mallory, served as the head coach at both Miami of Ohio and Indiana during his career. To this day he lives in Oxford, Ohio and got to know Hoeppner well during Hep's nineteen seasons at Miami.

One of Pont's favorite Hoeppner stories comes from the time leading up to Hep being hired at Indiana. Hoeppner knew that Pont was a good friend of Harold Mauro, a long-time coach and administrator at Indiana, and asked Pont if he would make a call on his behalf and ask two questions. He wanted to know exactly what Indiana expected from its head football coach, and what the salary would be – for his assistant coaches.

"The first part was easy," Pont said. "Indiana was looking for someone to go in there and reach out. They needed someone to be inclusive rather than exclusive. I told him he was going to need to go out into the communities, play a lot of golf, and find a way to get people on his side. When I asked Harold the second part of the question, he told me that I probably wouldn't believe it, but that assistant coaches at IU all made more than six figures per season. When I told Hep that, I think that sealed it for him. He was concerned, above all else, about making sure his guys were taken care of. That story tells me quite a bit about Terry Hoeppner. Not Hoeppner the head football coach, but Terry Hoeppner the person."

★ ★ ★

IU assistant coach Matt Canada tells a story about Hoeppner from a stressful month in Canada's life. As a member of Gerry DiNardo's coaching staff, Canada was hoping to stay on and be hired for Hoeppner's new IU staff. The interviews took place in the ten-day period following Hep's hiring. The problem was that Hoeppner's Miami team was playing in the Independence Bowl, so Canada figured his own assistant coaching future was probably not one of Hep's top priorities at that moment.

Canada soon found out he was wrong. Late afternoon the day of the Independence Bowl, Canada was out to dinner with his family when his cell phone rang. He didn't recognize the number, but the area code was "513" which meant it was from someone in Ohio. "I didn't think it was him, but I also answered the phone because I didn't have a job," Canada said. "But it was Hep, and I remember the conversation verbatim. He said, 'This is Terry Hoeppner,' and then went on to tell me that he had just stopped for some sweet tea at Chick-fil-A, which I found out later was something he always did. He wanted to offer me the quarterbacks coach and passing game coordinator job. I was shocked. It was everything I wanted to do."

To this day, Canada gets misty-eyed thinking about that conversation. "He was playing in a bowl game, and he certainly could have waited until the next day. But for him to call me and let me relax knowing that I had the job, and most of all, the job I wanted, was huge. He didn't have to do that, but I'm sure he was treating me the way he hoped he would be treated in a similar situation. That was Hep. He was always thinking about somebody else."

★ ★ ★

Franklin College always held a special place in Terry Hoeppner's heart. He played his college football there for Coach Red Faught, and later returned as an assistant for his mentor. From 1980-85, Hoeppner was Franklin's defensive coordinator before moving on to Miami in 1986.

Mike Leonard played at Hanover when Hoeppner coached at Franklin, and later attended many camps and clinics with Coach Hep. Eventually, Leonard would be adopted into the Franklin family as the Grizzlies' head football coach in 2003. Leonard came to Franklin with big aspirations of being the guy to turn around the program that first season. Five games in, however, Franklin was 0-5 and had just lost its Homecoming game. That night, Leonard went home feeling about as low as he possibly could. He was questioning his decision to take the Franklin job when his phone rang. His wife told him it was Miami of Ohio coach Terry Hoeppner on the line, and he wanted a little bit of Leonard's time.

"Here's the head coach at Miami of Ohio calling me at home to encourage me, knowing that we had gotten beat that day," Leonard said. "We talked about a book he was reading by John Gruden, *Do You Love Football?* He told me a story from that book about Gruden's rough first couple of games as the Raiders head coach. One of his assistants came into his office early in the morning and challenged Gruden with the question, 'Do you love football? Do you really love it? You love football, don't you?' That was kind of where I was. I was 0-5 and didn't really love football, and Hep was calling to tell me to keep plugging away. He said life's not easy, and football isn't easy sometimes. But he gave me this pep talk, and I've got to tell you I'll never forget that call for as long as I live. Every time I see that book, I think of Terry Hoeppner and it makes me smile."

★ ★ ★

Ken Beckley was the president of the Indiana University Alumni Association and head of the search committee formed in December of 2004 to look for a new football coach. After Hoeppner was hired, Beckley spent a great deal of time with Coach Hep going around the state speaking with alumni about Indiana football.

Beckley recalls one trip in particular that first summer, when they went to a cookout in Elkhart, Ind. at the home of an alumnus. He guesses there were about forty men in attendance. One in particular, a long-time Indiana supporter, listened to Hoeppner's spiel and then had a very pointed question for him. Basically, he said Hep's speech was all well and good, but he had heard it all before and nothing ever changed. Why should he think it would be any different with Coach Hep? "And Hep without hesitating said, 'Because we're going to win and this is going to work. But I have to have you on board,'" Beckley said. "And he said it with such conviction that everybody in the room knew it was going to happen. It wasn't going to happen overnight, but with Coach Hep it was going to happen."

Beckley echoed the many other assessments of Hoeppner as master salesman. "The number one thing in sales is to believe in your product, and he certainly believed in what he was selling," Beckley said. "If you don't believe in it, people can see through your eyes, and as I like to say, they can see through the tone of your voice. Hep was amazing in that regard. He was willing to go out and speak one-on-one with someone if he believed it could help make a difference. He'd convert the masses one at a time if necessary, and with Hep you knew he was serious."

★ ★ ★

Beckley also tells another story from Hoeppner's first spring as the Indiana coach in 2005. Coach Hep asked Indiana president Adam Herbert and Beckley to each coach one side in the annual spring game at Memorial Stadium. Beckley

165

said it was a "life highlight that he would ask me to do that."

Both Herbert and Beckley took their responsibilities very seriously that day. Beckley had mostly reserves on his team, and his Cream squad lost to the Crimson, 34-6, but he said he had a ball coaching the game. "We really wanted to win that game, but it obviously didn't work out that way," Beckley said. "But both teams were very into it and there was a lot of pride at stake. It was a thrill to get to be part of something like that, and it's something I will always treasure."

Beckley's participation in that game took his friendship with Hoeppner to a different level, too. From that night on, until the day he died, every time Hep saw Beckley he referred to him as "Coach Beckley." "That was pretty amazing," Beckley said. "From that day forward, he made me feel like one of the guys."

★ ★ ★

Many of Hoeppner's players at both Indiana and Miami considered their head coach a father figure. In many cases, Coach Hep filled a void for a player who didn't have a father in his life. But in the case of former Miami quarterback Ben Roethlisberger, who is very close to his father, Coach Hep became a second father figure.

Brenda Roethlisberger said that's simply the course their relationship took from the very start. "You can take your kids so far in life and then there have to be other people who play large roles. Coach Hep really picked up where we could no longer go. Ben was a man now, or at least becoming one very quickly, and even though his dad was there to give him advice, it's nice when you hear it a second time. My husband and Coach Hep really complemented each other well. We prayed for someone like Coach Hep all of those years to lead Ben to the next phase of his life. So he just kind of took over."

★ ★ ★

Karen Sampson, wife of Indiana basketball coach Kelvin Sampson, found it remarkable how much of an impact Terry

Hoeppner could have on people in such a short time. Sometime in 2006, Sampson's first year at IU, there was a function under a tented area outside of Memorial Stadium that both her husband and Hoeppner attended. Some of the Sampsons' close friends happened to be in town and briefly met Coach Hep that day. But they came away impressed with the IU football coach.

"I remember the day Coach Hep died, I called one of those friends and told her about it. She went on and on about how upset she was over the news and how it affected her personally. And this was after meeting this man for a total of five minutes. But I think that tells you a lot about the kind of person that Terry Hoeppner was. He didn't need to know you very long to make an impact on your life."

★ ★ ★

Indiana State Police trooper Curt Durnil has worked with IU football coaches since Cam Cameron took the Indiana job in 1997. His experiences with Cameron and Gerry DiNardo paved the way for his work with Coach Hep when he arrived on the scene in December of 2004. But there was one quality about Coach Hep that stood out above any other coach Durnil worked or played for (Durnil played both high school and college basketball) – his personality.

"There's no coach I've ever worked or played for who made me, or the guys around me, feel more welcome than Coach Hep," Durnil said. "The other coaches I worked with gave me everything I needed. But this guy made the person who emptied the trash cans at Memorial Stadium feel like he was part of the team. Coach Hep never met a stranger, and that's how he was different. He was a friend, and it was genuine. I really believed that Terry Hoeppner would be my friend for life. I said that many times. I was convinced that even after he was no longer the football coach here, we'd remain close friends, and in that way he was different, too."

★ ★ ★

Harold Mauro had been a part of Indiana University in some capacity for thirty-four years when Hoeppner got the IU job. He played for the Hoosiers and was on the '67 Rose Bowl team. He was an assistant coach on various IU football staffs and spent twenty-two years as a Senior Associate Athletic Director. But when Hep came on board, Mauro slid over and became IU's director of football operations.

One of his jobs was to help Hoeppner go around the state and promote Indiana football. That first summer when Hoeppner spoke to eighty-three different groups in an attempt to stir interest in IU football, Mauro was making the rounds, too. "We'd both go talk to the Kiwanis Clubs. He'd get the younger Kiwanis guys, and I'd always get the golden-age ones who would fall asleep after the first three sentences of my speech," Mauro said. "But I think I did more than forty that summer and he did more than eighty. He really got after it. We hit every dorm, sorority, fraternity, you name it. Anyone who wanted to talk Indiana football, we were ready to go. It was almost like we had our ankles taped before the season started. I did everything I could to keep up with him, but that was a monumental task."

✮ ✮ ✮

Terry Hoeppner made a difference. He got IU fans excited about Indiana football again. In at least one case, he got a Boilermaker, too. Dave, who describes himself as a 50-year-old Purdue alumnus, wrote a comment to the Hoosiers Insider blog at the *Indianapolis Star* the day Terry Hoeppner died. Even though he was a Boilermaker through and through, he had trouble not rooting for Hep as well.

"Only Terry Hoeppner could get me interested, even cheering, for the Hoosiers," Dave said in his blog comment. "Growing up in southeastern Indiana I was always a Miami of Ohio fan. When I sent my two kids to school there recently, I jumped back on the bandwagon, mostly because of Hep. What a great guy and coach. I hated to see him take the IU job for obvious reasons. It was the first time in my life I found myself wanting an IU athletic program to succeed. What a shame he could not see his mission through."

✯ ✯ ✯

The people who worked alongside Hoeppner in the IU athletic department have their stories, too. Anitra House, the director of eligibility and systems in the IU Compliance Department, was always impressed by the way Coach Hep recognized the efforts of everyone, no matter how small the tasks they performed. "When he needed to leave the football complex and come over to Assembly Hall for a meeting, he always made it a point to make the rounds visiting the offices and chatting with the staff briefly. It may have been just to say hi or thanks for some task fulfilled. He was never egotistical about his position, but I know he recognized how everyone appreciated the small piece of time he took to seek out others and express his interest and gratitude. Of course that behavior endeared him to the staff and made everyone want to work that much harder at whatever their small contribution might be to the larger operation in athletics."

✯ ✯ ✯

At Coach Hep's memorial service, assistant coach Joe Palcic told a story about how his head coach always put his team first. During the 2003 season at Miami, the RedHawks went on a 13-game winning streak. Every Tuesday after practice the coaches would order sub sandwiches from SDS Pizza. "About week four into the streak, Coach Hep came in and announced that he would like a chicken salad sub," Palcic recalled. "Bobby Johnson, our offensive line coach, asked him, 'But Coach, did you order a sub last week?' Hep did not. So we wouldn't let him order one that week either. Basically it was no subs for Coach Hep and he went hungry. Every week after that he would sit in the back of the room hungry while we all ate our subs. Coach Hep was always about what was best for the team."

✯ ✯ ✯

I debated about including a personal story or two in this book, but I certainly have my own favorite Hep stories from the two-and-a-half years that I knew him, covering Indiana University football for the *Indianapolis Star* while he was the coach. One that comes to mind occurred the day he was introduced as the Indiana coach. After the press conference I went to Rick Greenspan's home for his long-scheduled athletic department staff annual party.

Don Fischer and I were invited to the get-together and rode down together. I saw it as an extra opportunity to get some background on the new coach for the story I was writing the next day. When it was time for Hep to leave, Fischer and I were also leaving, so Fish offered to drop him and Jane at the Bloomington airport. They took him up on the offer, and we headed up State Road 37 for the 20-minute ride back up to Bloomington. But we did so in style.

Indiana State Police Trooper Curt Durnil gave us a police escort, with his lights flashing all the way to the airport. But what I remember from that ride more than traveling at high speeds on 37 was listening to Coach Hep go on and on from the back seat about how he was going to get this thing turned around. He definitely had a plan, and as he spoke, Jane just kept nodding her head in agreement because she knew how excited he was about the opportunity that was ahead. That was my first encounter with Coach Hep and one that I'll always have etched in my memory.

The other one that comes to mind happened in February of 2007, a few days after I learned that I had been named Sportswriter of the Year for the state of Indiana by the National Sportscasters and Sportswriters Association. One night around midnight I got a text message on my cell phone. It was from Hep, offering me his congratulations on my award. The message said he was out in Las Vegas for a function. "I just wanted you to know that I heard about your award all the way out here in Vegas, and I wanted to tell you how proud I was of your accomplishment." And I thought it was very cool that Coach Hep, with all of the other things he had going on, would take the time to drop me a quick message. I still have it saved in my phone, and I have no plans to erase it any time soon.

About the Author

Terry Hutchens has worked as a sportswriter for thirty years, including the past sixteen at the *Indianapolis Star* and the *Indianapolis News*. For the past ten years he has covered Indiana University football and basketball. In 2006, Terry was honored as Indiana's Sportswriter of the Year by the National Sportscasters and Sportswriters Association. This is Terry's second book. *Let 'Er Rip*, chronicling the Colts' improbable run to within one game of the Super Bowl, was published in 1995. Terry and his  wife Susan have been married twenty-one years and live in Indianapolis. They have two teenage sons, Bryan and Kevin.